MY DRUNKEN KITCHEN

A CELEBRATION OF THE JOYS OF DRINKING AND DINING

Helen Graves

DOG 'n' BONE

Published in 2014 by Dog 'n' Bone Books
An imprint of Ryland Peters & Small Ltd
20–21 Jockey's Fields   519 Broadway, 5th Floor
London WC1R 4BW   New York, NY 10012

www.rylandpeters.com

10 9 8 7 6 5 4 3 2 1

A CIP catalog record for this book is available from
the Library of Congress and the British Library.

ISBN: 978 1 909313 38 5

Printed in China

Editor: Rosie Lewis
Designer: Jerry Goldie
Illustrator: Kate Sutton

For digital editions, visit www.cicobooks.com/apps.php

Contents

Introduction

I'm going to have to kick things off with a disclaimer, because I don't want any legal action taken against me, and I'm guessing my publishers aren't crazy about the idea either. Really and truly, though, I don't want anyone to hurt themselves. Let me tell you a little story. I recently became known for writing on the subject of booze and cooking. People started commissioning me to write recipes here and there, an example being a mate's new cookbook, for which he issued me with the brief "please make a pissed sandwich" (I'm also known for my love of "serious" sandwiches). I was then asked to write a piece about "drunken cooking" for a London newspaper, and was photographed for it, whisk in one hand, wine glass and bottle in the other. The headline read "How to Make a Mean Pissed Pasta." A bit of fun, you might think? A bit of a laugh? Well, unfortunately, not for the London Fire Brigade. They slammed the article on their website, branding me "irresponsible" and "naive."

I hesitate to say that it really hacked me off, because, well, it's the fire brigade, innit? They save people's lives, they do a job of immeasurable value. THEY SAVE PEOPLE'S LIVES. I couldn't argue with them in any way, ever. What I wanted to point out, though, in a really tiny voice (or maybe shout from the bar tops), was that it was meant as a joke. Anyone with half a brain cell knows they shouldn't actually be cooking when, as I think I rather eloquently put it in the article, "completely ratted." Don't

they? Surely? I guess not everyone is as intelligent as us, huh. Still, as I said, I wouldn't argue with the fire brigade. The next day they thanked me for being such a "good sport," by which I assume they meant "thanks for not getting upset while we made an example out of you and put you on the receiving end of a huge amount of abuse on Twitter." They offered to come and give me a fire safety lesson in my kitchen, to which I responded "Please come in uniform." Funnily enough, I didn't hear from them again.

Playing with fire

Clearly I also have a reputation for being a little silly now and again, but really, I am serious on this point. Allow me to further illustrate the stupidity of cooking while utterly hosed, by way of a story from a friend. In his words:

> A mate of mine from an old job woke up one morning with a terrible hangover, when the doorbell rang. He answered it, and after standing silent for a couple of seconds a woman he swore he'd never seen before said "You don't remember me, do you?" Turns out he'd got trashed the night before and attempted to cook some bacon on the gas stove. He was so trashed, though, that while sitting on the sofa waiting for it to cook, he passed out. This woman had, a good while later, been passing his house on the way home from work and noticed 4-foot flames lighting up his kitchen from the pan of burning bacon fat. She rang the doorbell but got no answer, and was about to call the fire brigade when she noticed that in his pissed state, he had left the front door open. So she went in and tried to wake him, and when that didn't do anything, she calmly placed a damp dish towel over the pan, turned the gas off, and left.

It's a funny story, but there's no denying that guy had a serious stroke of luck. I cannot guarantee that you will have such a helpful person passing your house at exactly the right time of night (I also can't promise you that you won't get robbed because you left your front door open). So. The point I am trying to make is that you should not be needing the fire brigade as a result of this book. I don't want anyone ever to need them, particularly not as a result of their own stupidity. We don't want the hospital involved either, so please, if you are completely hosed, do not hesitate to visit that takeout, or, ideally, drink a pint of water and get yourself to bed.

Moving On

So that's the boring bit over, yes? We can have all the fun now? I'm excited. We will romp, careen, sizzle, and souse our way

through some boozy culinary scenarios of varying intensity. We will take a tongue-in-cheek, sideways glance at the relationship between food and booze; at the effects the latter has on the appetite and the taste buds, and also at the ways it can actually, genuinely, improve your cooking. You'll have to bear with me on that one.

I want you to know, too, that there is more to the drunken kitchen than late-night fridge fumbling or takeout dodging (although of course I won't let you down in those areas). We will also explore the joys of the drunken daytime cooking session, something I feel is hugely underappreciated. There's a look at a vision of the perfect pub, and let us not forget that booze is good for cooking with as well as drinking, so there will be a bit of that as well. I will also be there for you the morning after (in the form of soothing recipes—I'm not coming round), with contributions from professional chefs and proprietors of top restaurants, who know a thing or 400 about cooking and boozing. Chefs are a hedonistic lot in general, so if anyone knows how to cook their way out of a hangover, they do. We're going to cover all the angles, basically, and just in case you're left wanting more, I've provided a handy Further Reading section as a nightcap.

Things to note

Let me just point out a few things to bear in mind as you read through this book:

1 Serving sizes are provided as number of servings rather than number of people served because, to the drunk or hungover person, the average serving size is generally completely inadequate and therefore meaningless.

2 As a piece of general cooking advice, it's best to read the recipe and get all your ingredients out and ready beforehand, but in the drunken kitchen, this is pretty much crucial.

3 Don't walk away from the kitchen or leave anything unattended at any time. PLEASE. Again, this is good general advice.

4 Never, ever consider deep-frying when even mildly inebriated. You won't find any recipes requiring you to do that in this book, for good reason (see the bit about the fire brigade, above).

So harness that thirst, readers. Let me get the first round in. Bottoms up. Gloves off. Ding ding. (Okay, I'll stop now.)

CHAPTER 1

The Daytime Drunk

A Creative Catalyst

Daytime drinking is to creativity in the kitchen as psychoactive substances were to Aldous Huxley's *Doors of Perception*. In other words, a lunchtime drinky does wonders for freeing one from the shackles of anxiety about culinary experimentation.

Picture the scene

Let us imagine that you have a day off work, a day off being preferable to a weekend because it enhances the feeling of naughtiness when we get down to the drinking. This works even better as a scenario, actually, if you start out mildly hungover, because it allows for the introduction of the "hair of the dog" drink, which can often lead to the best kind of tipsy drunk ever. Let's imagine that you were out the night before. It got late, you were fairly inebriated, your mate missed the last train home and so ended up staying at your place. This means that he or she is there in the morning (hopefully; if not, you might want to check the doorstep), you're both feeling it a bit, but you're there to pull each other through. Lunchtime arrives and oh, hang on, what's this? There's a little devil on your shoulder, speaking suggestive things into your hot, sensitive ears. "You know what would really make you feel tip-top just now, don't you? Yes. Yessss. A nice cold, fizzy beer; something sprightly and kicking with life. Hoppy, but with hardcore citrus notes to send a scaffolding pole right up your spine, lifting you off the sofa and back to the land of the cooking." He's quite a verbose little devil, apparently.

Good, wasn't it? That beer, I mean. Almost makes you fancy another. Before you know it, you're three-quarters of the way into the second, and wahey! the stomach starts to rumble. This is it. Don't miss this chance, for it is the optimum time to get busy in the kitchen.

And so it begins

A little daytime drinking is fun because it feels wrong and slightly delinquent, which means it's automatically more enjoyable. Ah, the power of the guilty pleasure. That is, after all, what this book is all about. A side effect of feeling that you are doing something you really—technically speaking and according to the rules of civilized society—shouldn't, is the arrival of a new and special kind of creativity, a sort of "to hell with it" attitude, that allows a cook to forget what it is that "usually" or, worse, "normally" would be added to a recipe. For example, you might ordinarily stand agonizing over whether or not it was 3 fl oz (100 ml) of fizzy water in the batter for the Korean chicken wings, but not the tipsy daytime cook. Oh no. This cook slings caution to the wind and throws in half the can of beer they are holding, instantly creating a more flavorsome batter. Yes, I am aware that this isn't the craziest of examples, but don't be pedantic; you get the gist.

Crisp Omelet

Allow me to illustrate further the thought process touched on overleaf with an example of a recipe: the crisp omelet.[*] Now now, stay with me. You think I've lost it at this point; I can sense your faces screwing up into crumpled confusion. Crisps? In an omelet? I know, right? Well how about if I told you that the inventor and inspration for this concept has also been repeatedly voted one of the world's greatest chefs? Huh? Sounding more interesting now? Maybe not, but I'm going to tell you anyway.

The chef is Ferran Adrià, whose restaurant, El Bulli in Catalonia, Spain (which closed in 2011), had three Michelin stars. Okay, so El Bulli was famous for serving extremely experimental food, some of which was actually inedible according to a friend of mine who managed to get tickets one year via the highly competitive lottery system, but that's not the point. The point is that Adrià was not constrained by convention, and this state of mind led him to produce some highly innovative cooking. The crisp omelet came from his "home cooking" recipe book, which, I am told, was a little more accessible but no less curious. This recipe might sound bonkers, but think about it: the salty crisps season the omelet and bring some interesting texture to the dish; the center is dense and chewy where the crisps have soaked up the egg mixture, yet the bits poking out the top are all, well, still crisp.

I think everyone should give this recipe a go at least once, if only to get into the spirit of the experimental kitchen. After that, the world is your sous-vide oyster with raspberry-jam dip and a chicken-skin garnish.

---

[*] Sorry US pals, we're doing this the UK way and referring to potato chips as crisps. However, in the interests of balance, international diplomacy, and to maintain that "special relationship" we'll spell omelette your way.

6 eggs

1 packet cheese and onion crisps (potato chips), 1 packet ready salted crisps

A generous pat (knob) of butter

A handful of grated cheddar cheese, or perhaps two handfuls. I'd say two

Freshly ground black pepper

Chili sauce, to serve

Makes 4 servings

1 In a large bowl, beat the eggs lightly, then add the crisps (chips) and add a grind of black pepper.

2 Heat the butter in a heavy frying pan and add the crisp and egg mixture. Allow the omelet to cook over a medium heat for a few minutes, tilting the pan to fill any holes and to ensure even eggy coverage.

3 When almost set on top (with just a thin layer of uncooked egg remaining), sprinkle on the cheese, fold over, and serve. I like a blob of chili sauce on the side. Chili sauce is a good friend to the drunken cook.

Sandwiches

So you're channeling your inner Aldous now, right? The creative spirit has hopefully been unleashed, and it's time to get involved with one of my favorite topics, which also happens to be one of the most popular lunches in the Western world: sandwiches. I am serious about sandwiches. I've written an entire book about them, and I've got my mind on writing another. You probably don't know it, but you've been releasing that inner creative for years through the medium of the sandwich. To use the example of, er, crisps (chips), once again (highbrow stuff, this), you were getting into the zone way back when you started putting your crisps into your sandwich at school. It made things a whole lot more exciting, didn't it? The keruuuunch of the crisps as you press down on the bread; the pinball effect in the mouth as salty meets sharp meets crisp meets soft cheese or ham and fluffy bread. It's a taste sensation! You never looked back. If you've not put your crisps in a sandwich since childhood, then I urge you to give it a go. Anyway, this book is not called Recipes with Crisps; I am merely illustrating a point. Sandwiches offer a good starting platform for the daytime drunk, and here are two gloriously deviant numbers I came up with myself whilst either inebriated or hungover.

Candied Bacon Eggy Bread Sandwich

I'll be honest, this has been more of a fixture in my hungover kitchen than I care to think about, let alone admit. I say this makes two servings because it really is incredibly intense. There's the sweet saline kinkiness of the candied bacon for a start, but to put it between two egg-soaked pieces of bread that have been fried in butter—well, I'm patting myself on the back right now. I'll leave this one with you as it's not for the fainthearted. You'll think I'm either sick, or a genius. Perhaps a sick genius.

4 slices streaky bacon

Light brown sugar

1 egg

A splash of milk

2 slices white bread

A large pat (knob) of butter

Salt and freshly ground black pepper

Makes 2 servings

1 Preheat the oven to 400°F (200°C, Gas 8) and lay out the bacon slices on a baking sheet. Sprinkle with the sugar so that they are lightly coated all over, and cook for 6–8 minutes.

2 Turn them over, sprinkle with sugar again, and cook for a further 6–8 minutes, until they are a lovely dark-brown color. Watch them like a hawk to make sure they don't catch and burn. Remove onto a wire rack (DO NOT USE YOUR FINGERS) and allow to cool until hard. This won't take long.

3 Whisk the egg with the milk and season highly with salt and pepper. Melt the butter in a frying pan. Dip a slice of bread into the eggy milk mixture, making sure it really soaks the liquid up, and fry until brown on both sides.

4 Use the eggy bread to sandwich the bacon. Say goodbye to your self-respect.

2 frozen potato
waffles

5 slices streaky bacon

2 slices cheese, such
as Gruyère (you want
a good melter,
basically)

2 eggs

A splash of milk

1¾ oz (50 g) butter,
for frying

Salt

Confectioners' (icing)
sugar, for dusting

Maple syrup, for
drizzling

Makes 1 serving

Bacon, Cheese, and Maple Syrup Wafflewich

This is good for the daytime drinker who finds themselves on a brunchy vibe, and could potentially work well in the hangover scenario, should you have sufficient surviving cognitive ability to deal with this sweet and salty mind-bender. Potato waffles—another ingredient that might transport you back to childhood—make an appearance here. I promise we'll get slightly more sophisticated, but for now just get down with the nostalgia. Anyway, drunk people essentially are like children, so it makes perfect sense.

1 Cook the waffles according to the packet instructions (in case you don't know, you can cook them in a toaster if yours has a frozen setting—it's much faster and less hassle).

2 Broil (grill) the bacon until crisp, then place it on a cooked waffle. Put the cheese on top, sprinkle with a little salt, and seal with the second waffle.

3 Beat the eggs with the milk and pour into a large, shallow dish (you need to be able to dip the whole sandwich into it). Melt the butter in a heavy frying pan.

4 Dip the sandwich into the egg mixture, turn it over so that both sides are coated, and put it into the pan. Cook until golden brown on one side, then flip to cook the other side, weighing the sandwich down with a heavy object, such as another pan (if you don't have one you can just press it down).

5 Remove to a plate, then dust with confectioners' (icing) sugar and zigzag with maple syrup. Filthbag.

Waffle Alternatives

Tempting as it may be, don't just limit yourself to cheese and bacon when choosing a filling for your wafflewich. Here's a few alternatives you might like to try:

- Fried eggs

- Steak and eggs

- Beans, cheese, and eggs

- More bacon

- Even more bacon

CHAPTER 2

The Late-night Drunk

The Classic Scenario

When I started planning this book, I wanted to make absolutely sure that it wasn't just going to be about going out, getting lashed, coming home, and cooking some junk. I didn't want that because firstly, that's a pretty lame idea for a whole book, but secondly—importantly—as I said in the introduction, I see the drunken kitchen as so much more than that. It's about more than doing your best with a packet of instant noodles. I'm not saying I'm against that; I'm just saying there are other ways. Also, noodle pimpage is something I've written about in several other places and, seriously, a woman's gotta move on. The idea also brings to mind a friend's rather desperate ritual of drunken noodling, which plays out thus: "I purchase a pack of instant noodles (chicken curry) and cheddar cheese. I get home, cook the noodles, get annoyed that I've put too much water in, then grate the cheese over the top before sloshing liberally with chili sauce. It tastes bloody odd and yet I keep doing it. I don't know why." Tragic, I think you'll agree.

Turn away from the dark side

Come with me, readers, beyond the land of drunken packet noodles, past the goblin kingdom, and toward the point of light that is the revolutionized late-night cooking session. It's tricky to get right. I'll cover substitutes for crappy takeouts in the next chapter, but for now, I want to go in a slightly different direction with some ideas for late-night spot-hitters that you might not have previously considered. I'm pretty confident that, as adults, you really don't need someone to tell you how to come home from the bar or pub, raid the cupboards, and make, hmmm, I dunno, a toasted cheese sandwich.

Mmm, toasted cheese sandwich.

Tasty, yes, but you've been doing that for years, and I'm guessing you're reading this book because you're interested in other options; you're curious and excited, perhaps, to realize the true potential of the late-night kitchen. Good. This will happen. The reason we must exercise slight caution is that this is when you are most likely to have imbibed a fair whack. I advise against over-ambition. You'll find, therefore, that these recipes are nice and simple, yet far from boring. Let's mix it up a little, then, and make like the Japanese, with a recipe for okonomiyaki.

Okono-what?

If you're not familiar, the okonomiyaki is a Japanese savory sort-of-eggy pancake that may contain, well, quite a lot of things. The name of the dish comes partly from "okonomi," which means "what you want" and can basically include whatever you have to hand. Urgh, I hate it when people say that. No, it can be made with any number of ingredients that taste good in okonomiyaki. The base is cabbage, which, I admit, is not very high up on the list of ingredients to stimulate the drunken appetite, but when it is cooked with other fillings, such as shrimp (prawns) or pork, and topped with strongly flavored garnishes, its role becomes clear: it provides structure and texture to the eggy mix. Anyway, you eat shredded cabbage in your kebabs, so get over it.

Okonomiyaki

This is a fun dish for the drunk cook to tackle, because it allows for liberation of the inner "artist." I don't want to be clichéd and suggest you channel Jackson Pollock, but it's hard to think of a better example. Of course, it's not at all insulting to compare the work of one of the most important Abstract Expressionists to something you made by squeezing sauce from a bottle when drunk, so we're fine. The two essential sauces here are okonomiyaki sauce (like sweet Worcestershire sauce) and Japanese (sweetened) mayo; yes, it sounds bonkers, but I promise you it works. Anyway, you're drunk, you should be bang up for anything. Oh, and I've provided substitutes for both sauces in the recipe below, in case you can't find them, so don't think you're getting out of it that easily.

There are two main styles of okonomiyaki: Osaka and Hiroshima. This is a recipe for the former. It doesn't contain noodles, like the Hiroshima version, but there's nothing to stop you eating noodles with it if you want to get crazy. Just stay away from the grated cheese, okay?

3½ oz (100 g) all-purpose (plain) flour

5½ fl. oz (160 ml) water

8½ oz (250 g) white cabbage, core removed, leaves finely sliced and cut into short lengths (this should be about ¼ cabbage)

3 scallions (spring onions), finely sliced

4½ oz (125 g) shrimp (prawns)

1 heaped tbsp pickled ginger, sliced into thin strips

2 large eggs, beaten

1 tbsp vegetable oil

4 slices streaky bacon, cut into 1 in (2.5 cm) lengths

Okonomiyaki sauce (or use 2 tbsp ketchup mixed with 2 tbsp Worcestershire sauce)

Japanese mayonnaise (or mix 3½ oz/100 g mayonnaise with 1 tbsp rice vinegar or white wine vinegar and a pinch of sugar until the sugar dissolves)

Bonito flakes (optional)

Salt and freshly ground black pepper

Makes 4 servings

1 You will need an ovenproof frying pan or skillet (i.e. one that can go under the broiler/grill without melting). Whisk the flour with the water until you have a smooth batter. Add the cabbage and scallions (spring onions) to the batter, along with the shrimp (prawns), pickled ginger, and a good pinch of salt (a bit more salt than you think is reasonable).

2 Add the eggs and stir everything to combine, but do not overmix. Set the ovenproof frying pan over a medium heat and add the oil, spreading it evenly over the surface of the pan (this is easy with a piece of kitchen paper). Tip the mixture into it and flatten it out into a circle. Arrange the bacon on top. Cook for 8 minutes.

3 Now, at this stage the okonomiyaki would usually be flipped, but that's asking way too much from the drunken cook. Trust me, I've tested all these recipes. Instead, put the frying pan under a medium broiler (grill) and cook for another 10–15 minutes, or until cooked through and really golden on top. The bacon should be beautifully crisp. Remove from the grill.

4 Now's your artistic moment: squiggle the surface first with okonomiyaki sauce, then with the Japanese mayo. Top with a conservative handful of bonito flakes, if you like. Allow to cool for 5 minutes then serve, in fat wedges.

Patty Melt on a K-Tip

I know this is kind of like a toasted cheese sandwich, but it's really a patty melt, so ha! A patty melt with a soft spot for K-pop. In case you've never had a patty melt, it's like a burger that's sandwiched between slices of bread with loads of cheese and then fried … like, er, a toasted cheese sandwich. I promise it's still not one, though. A drunken palate demands the most explosive of taste sensations, which brings me to kimchi, or spicy Korean fermented cabbage, aka one of the world's finest condiments. It works in this sandwich for three reasons: 1) the crunch of cabbage adds pleasing textural contrast; 2) chili is beloved of drunk people; 3) the fermentation gives the cabbage blue cheese-like flavors that work very well with the beef.

5 oz (150 g) good ground (minced) beef (not lean)

2 slices decent white sourdough bread or other sturdy white bread (it must be able to hold the filling. This is a juicy sandwich; cheap bread will disintegrate)

A large pat (knob) of butter. Oh yes

2 tbsp kimchi

3 or 4 slices processed cheese (yes, processed works best here. Feel free to change it—it's your kitchen, after all.)

Salt and freshly ground black pepper

Makes 1 serving

1 Form the beef into a patty roughly the same size and shape as a slice of the bread. Don't worry too much about getting it exactly right.

2 Heat a heavy frying pan or preferably a cast-iron skillet until very hot (but not smoking). Season the patty really well on the outside with salt and pepper. Put it in the pan and cook for 2 minutes on each side. Don't attempt to move it before the 2 minutes is up, because it will stick. Once it is cooked, place it on one slice of bread.

3 Turn down the heat to medium-low and melt the butter in the pan. Top the patty with the kimchi, followed by the cheese, and the other slice of bread.

4 Place the sandwich into the pan and fry until golden brown and crisp (have a look after a minute or so). If you have another heavy pan, put it on top to weigh the sandwich down. Otherwise, just press it. Flip it and repeat until golden on the other side, and serve immediately.

Chickpea Smash

This dish is based on falafel; it has the same spicing and saucing but none of the deep-frying. See how I look after you? There's still some frying, though—don't worry, I'm not trying to make this healthy or anything. (Rolls eyes.) There's cheese to make damn sure it isn't.

For the chickpeas

3 tbsp olive oil, plus extra for drizzling

1 red onion, finely diced

3 cloves of garlic, crushed

1 level tsp ground cumin

¾ level tsp ground coriander

1 tsp chili flakes

1 can chickpeas, drained and rinsed (6½ oz/180 g drained weight)

Juice of ½ lemon

A handful of fresh parsley leaves, chopped

A handful of cilantro (coriander) leaves, chopped

Salt and freshly ground black pepper

For the rest

About 7 oz (200 g) halloumi, sliced

2 pita breads

Pickled chilies, sliced

Hummus

Cucumber slices

Pickled chilies, sliced

Shredded iceberg lettuce

Makes 2 servings

1 Heat 3 tbsp of olive oil in a frying pan and cook the onion until soft but not colored. Add the garlic and cook for a couple of minutes, stirring.

2 Add the ground spices and chili flakes and cook for a couple more minutes, stirring. Be careful not to burn the spices. Add the chickpeas and fry them in the spiced onion mixture for 5 minutes or so, until nicely warmed through.

3 Meanwhile, place the halloumi slices in a dry pan and turn the heat up fairly high. Cook for few minutes each side or until golden brown. Put the pita on to toast.

4 Using a fork or potato masher, crush the chickpea mixture roughly—you want to leave some chickpeas whole and crush others lightly.

5 Squeeze in the lemon juice, sprinkle with the parsley and cilantro (coriander), and season with salt and pepper. Add a slug of olive oil and stir to combine.

6 Split the pita and spread with hummus. Add half the chickpea mixture and top with the halloumi. Top with cucumber, pickled chilies, and iceberg lettuce. Repeat with the other pita. Serve immediately.

Chipotle and Mushroom Quesadillas

There can never be enough ways to consume melted cheese, right? Right. If you can get Mexican cheese easily (hi America!), do use it here. I like the way the Mexican cheeses go melty but don't have a dominant flavor, so you can whack a large amount in there. Cheddar works very well too, though, and personally I'm down with a nice bit of maturity in a cheese. Chipotle chilies are a key ingredient for the drunk kitchen as they have great depth of flavor and impart a sort of magical smokiness to anything and everything.

1 tbsp vegetable oil

1 onion, diced

1 red bell pepper, diced

3 cloves of garlic, crushed

6 chestnut (or other) mushrooms, sliced

6 chipotles in adobo (or to taste), finely (ish) chopped

14 oz (400 g) can chopped tomatoes

4 tortillas

8½ oz (250 g) queso fresco, other Mexican cheese, or cheddar, grated

4 scallions (spring onions), finely sliced

Salt and freshly ground black pepper

Makes 2 quesadillas

1 Heat the oil and soften the onion and bell pepper over a medium heat until the onion is translucent, about 5–10 minutes. Add the garlic for the last minute or so.

2 Add the mushrooms, chipotles (plus any sauce that came with them), tomatoes, and salt and pepper. Cook for 15 minutes, or until the sauce has thickened (you don't want excess juice in your quesadillas).

3 Heat a dry frying pan over a medium-low heat and add a tortilla, put a quarter of the cheese on top, then spread over a layer of the sauce mixture. Add another quarter of the cheese on top, then sprinkle on half the scallions (spring onions). Put the other tortilla on top and press down.

4 When golden underneath (it won't take long), flip the whole thing over and cook until the other side is golden. Remove from the pan, cut into wedges, and serve. Repeat with the remaining ingredients to make another quesadilla.

XinJiang Lamb Noodles

This recipe is based loosely on one from my favorite local restaurant, Silk Road in southeast London. Their cumin lamb skewers are legendary, and their cumin lamb noodles are so fiery and salty that, well, let's just say there's always a price to pay and it isn't just a fiscal one. My version is a little more accessible. It would be right and proper to use hand-pulled noodles here, but let's face it, that is never going to happen in this scenario. I've used udon, which will send noodle purists into cardiac arrest, but this is the only noodle that is easily available yet has the right amount of satisfying chew. It tastes good, so the food police can do one.

8½ oz (250 g) lamb leg steak, thinly sliced

1½ tsp cumin seeds

1 tsp ground cumin

1 tsp chili flakes

2 cloves of garlic, crushed

1 tbsp rice wine vinegar or sherry

1 tsp light soy sauce

1 tsp dark soy sauce

1 tsp cornstarch (cornflour) mixed with 1 tsp water

2 tbsp oil

½ onion, thickly sliced

½ green bell pepper, coarsely chopped

3½ oz (100 g) fresh udon noodles

Chili oil, to serve

Makes 1 serving

1 Combine the lamb, cumin seeds, ground cumin, chili flakes, garlic, rice wine vinegar, light and dark soy, and cornstarch (cornflour) mixture in a bowl.

2 Heat half the oil in a wok and stir-fry the onion and bell pepper for a couple of minutes until lightly charred. Set aside on a plate.

3 Add the rest of the oil and half the lamb. Stir-fry for a few minutes, or until the lamb is just cooked. Set aside.

4 Repeat with the other half of the lamb, then add all the meat, vegetables, and noodles to the wok. Stir-fry until everything is hot, and serve with chili oil.

Sick Spaghetti

I was going to give you a recipe that would have made an Italian nonna wince. I imagine. Certainly, anyone with any respect for pasta would not have been happy with it. To elaborate: there are many recipes floating around for "all-in-one pasta," which involves cooking pasta and all the sauce ingredients in one pot, at the same time. What a curious idea, I thought. Potentially perfect for the drunken cook! The idea is that you throw everything into a pan, then, 10 minutes and a lot of stirring later, the lot is transformed into perfectly sauced pasta. Except that isn't what actually happens. I don't think I've ever been so horrified during a recipe-testing session than I was when I beheld the finished product. A claggy, gloopy tangle of starch with the most unpleasant texture. Someone should be arrested. And all to save on one pan! That must be the reason, right? Who can't be bothered to cook pasta in one pan and a basic sauce in the other, and mix them together? It seems to me that one-pan pasta is trying to solve a problem that doesn't exist, and I'm telling you about it purely for the purposes of closure.

Phew. What you are getting instead is a tried-and-tested stalwart from my drunk kitchen: sick spaghetti. I call it so because it contains excessive amounts of butter and anchovies. It contains a whole can of anchovies, in fact. I make no apologies for that.

More pasta than is considered acceptable for two people, say 10½ oz (300 g)

A large pat (knob) of butter (a lot more than you think is necessary)

2 oz (50 g) can anchovies

2 cloves of garlic, crushed

1 red chili, sliced (or chili flakes, to taste)

Juice of ½ lemon

A handful of fresh parsley leaves (or basil for any spicy renegades), finely chopped

Salt and freshly ground black pepper

Makes 2 servings

1 Pour yourself a large glass of wine.

2 Cook the pasta according to the packet instructions in a large pan of salted water (ideally for a couple of minutes less than advised on the packet, but you're drunk, so do your best).

3 In a small pan, melt the butter. Drain the anchovies and whack them into the pan. Mash them about a bit until they start to melt and break up.

4 Wang in the crushed garlic and chili and fry gently without burning it. Squeeze in the lemon juice.

5 Drain the pasta, put it back in the pan, and mix with the sauce. Add pepper and parsley, and serve.

One-pot Wonders

Pasta is an obvious choice for a drunk cook and a good one—when ingested it soaks up booze both before and after eating. It's easy to mess up, though, so follow these rules:

- Always add either a lot of butter or a lot of olive oil

- Always add more garlic than you think is reasonable

- Ditto chilli

In fact, spaghetti with olive oil and garlic is a real dish and one of the tastiest you can knock up in the time it takes to, well, cook some pasta, actually.

CHAPTER 3

Takeaway Dodging

There is Another Way

I visit my fair share of takeouts, but not when I'm drunk. Not any more. And no, I'm not just saying that. The late-night, post-bar or club takeout experience is something I left behind a long time ago, but I can recall the experiences very clearly. The stumbling approach, the sudden, cruel strip lighting, the odd couple arguing outside. Someone slumped against the window, kebab spilled down their front. The honk of fried chicken on the vomit comet. Garlic sauce with its whiff of garlic powder that's fine at the time but leaves an aftertaste like nothing else: an acrid, sour twang. Chili sauce that's never hot enough. The overload of shredded cabbage. The post-kebab feeling of shame. What? Surely everyone has had a similar experience? Perhaps you're all too classy ever to have frequented such a place.

In bed with my dinner

Have you ever woken up next to a kebab? I have. Sorry mum. Once is enough, take it from me. Anyone who has done this knows that the smell of cold, fatty meat lingers in a room far

longer than any other smell ever. I was a teenager, obviously, and have since learned to drink more responsibly. I also generally aim to stay awake around my food. What I'm trying to say is that these recipes are the opposite—well, an alternative, anyway—to face-palming a 'bab and waking up with a pickled chili stuck to your nose. If you think you may still be in that phase, I suggest you stop reading and go order another fluorescent alcopop. Or something.

Dodging ... The Shonky Kebab

It's almost a cliché nowadays to use the phrase "elephant's leg" to describe the average kebab, but it does perfectly evoke that specific category of grilled protein. The rotating cylinder of compacted meat, each air-exposed layer shaved off by a long, thin knife and deposited into pappy pita by disposable-gloved hands. It always seems like a good idea at the time.

It isn't, though. Not really. The kebab recipe below is what I would call "proper," and is for those who have graduated to the world of "adult drinking." It is for those who want food that actually tastes nice. The secret to these kebabs is that they contain surprisingly few ingredients, which means that the flavors stay distinct. The dates add welcome nubbins of sweetness; they're my secret kebab weapon. Well, they were until I wrote this, anyway. The melted ghee is optional, but it does make for particularly juicy, decadent kebabs, and who doesn't ever want melted butter involved?

The salad is adapted from a recipe by Nigella Lawson, and is a great accompaniment to loads of grilled meats, but particularly lamb (the pomegranate and cumin work particularly well with a bit of sheep). Don't skip it.

Lamb and Date Kebabs

For the kebabs

½ onion, peeled

8½ oz (250 g) ground (minced) lamb

2 cloves of garlic, crushed

2 green chilies, finely chopped

1 tsp red chili powder

1 tsp garam masala

A small handful of cilantro (coriander) leaves, roughly chopped

1 egg

2 dates, pitted and finely chopped

Melted butter or ghee, for basting the kebabs

Salt and freshly ground black pepper

1 In a bowl, combine the pomegranate juice, lime juice, and sliced onion for the salad. Set aside.

2 To make the kebabs, chop or process the onion finely and lay it out on a sheet of kitchen paper to soak up the excess moisture while you mix together all the other kebab ingredients, except the dates and ghee. Season.

3 Now get your hands in there and knead the meat for about 5 minutes, as you would bread. Smoosh it against the bottom of the bowl. Do not skip this step, as it is essential for the texture, and I do mean essential.

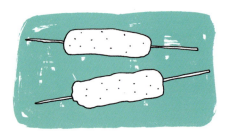

For the salad

Seeds and juice of
½ pomegranate

Juice of 1 lime

1 red onion, sliced

A handful each of fresh
mint, parsley, and
cilantro (coriander)
leaves

A pinch of ground
cumin

Salt and freshly ground
black pepper

To serve

Flatbreads

Natural yogurt

Makes 2 servings

4 When you've finished kneading, stir in the dates. It's important to add them last, otherwise they will break up and make the entire mixture sweet, which is not what we're looking for.

5 Shape the mixture into 4 sausages (around skewers if you like, although I don't usually bother), and broil (grill) for 5–6 minutes each side or until cooked through, basting occasionally with the melted ghee.

6 Add the pomegranate seeds, herbs, ground cumin, and salt and pepper to the onion mixture and stir well to combine. Warm the flatbreads and stuff each with a kebab, salad, and yogurt. Stuff into face.

Dodging ... The Skanky Pizza

Lahmacun is pronounced lah-mah-jun, in case you didn't know. I want you to be up to speed with your takeout replacement lingo. This is the kind of information you can use to impress your mates, as you watch them wolf down what is surely one of the tastiest snacks in the entire world. The lahmacun is from Turkey, and some people—imaginatively—call it "Turkish pizza," because it looks a little bit like—wait for it—a pizza. It's not, though, it's a flatbread smeared with a really pokey combination of ground (minced) lamb or beef and chili, then rolled up around a herb-heavy salad and eaten at something approaching the speed of light because it is so unspeakably delicious.

Lahmacun

½ red bell pepper

½ onion

1 green chili

10½ oz (300 g) ground (minced) lamb

3 cloves of garlic, crushed

1 tbsp tomato paste

1 tsp ground cumin

2 tsp chili flakes, or to taste (Turkish chili flakes are great here, but you can substitute regular chili flakes)

1 tsp paprika

4 flatbreads

Salt

To serve

Fresh lemon juice

Parsley

Sliced onion

Pickled turnips or cucumbers, or both

Chili flakes (optional)

Natural yogurt

Makes 4 servings

1 Finely chop the bell pepper, onion, and green chili—the easiest way is to pulse them in a blender or food-processor. Don't overblend—you don't want mush.

2 Once chopped, mix with the meat and all the other topping ingredients, and season with salt. Give it a really good mix using your hands. Divide the mixture equally between the 4 flatbreads, spreading it right to the edges.

3 Place under a medium hot broiler (grill) until the lamb is cooked through and the flatbreads crisping at the edges.

4 Sprinkle each lahmacun with lemon juice, then top with parsley leaves, slices of onion, and pickles, plus extra chili flakes if you like. Add a dollop of yogurt, roll up, and insert into face.

Dodging ... The Sad Fries

I'm including this recipe as a halfway house between getting a takeout and doing it yourself. I'm also including it because I understand that some of you won't be able to get by without fries, and, as I said at the beginning of the book, there will be no deep-frying in the drunken kitchen. So you're going to have to buy your fries, but then take 'em home and pimp 'em. Uh-huh. This is an idea I pinched from a street-food van in London called "The Grilling Greek." Their fries were such a revelation that I had to make my own. You'd think the feta would be a bit rubbish on the hot fries, sort of rubbery and inappropriate, but no, it's part solid, part melty, and it spreads itself all around those fries in little crumbles that you can scoop feverishly from the bottom of the dish with your fingers. The rosemary and chipotle salt obviously matches very well; that's an idea I pinched from a burger restaurant. I know—I'm nothing if not original. It's a piece of cake to make, too, and you can use it on loads of stuff, including roast lamb, chicken, or potatoes, or with focaccia and olive oil, or ... You get the idea: it goes with lots of things.

Pimped Rosemary, Chili, and Feta Fries

3 sprigs rosemary, leaves stripped

1 dried chipotle chili, seeds shaken out, roughly chopped

10½ oz (300 g) sea salt

Zest of ½ lemon

7 oz (200 g) feta cheese

1 portion of fries

White wine vinegar, for sprinkling

Portion sizes will vary depending on how many fries you have

1 Put the rosemary leaves, chipotle chili, and half the salt into a blender or food processor and pulse until well mixed. Stir in the rest of the salt and the lemon zest.

2 Crumble the feta over the hot fries and sprinkle with the rosemary salt and white wine vinegar. Fancy.

Dodging ... The Crappy Curry

There must be a speedy curry recipe in this book; of course there must. This did, however, present me with two problems. The first is with so many amazing curries in the world, it's impossible to choose just one. Which would be the most popular? The way to find out, of course, was to ask Twitter. My research was nothing if not rigidly scientific. Surely the most popular answer should be the recipe that is needed for this book. I say "needed" because I am obviously providing an important public service here. The problem was, you all said different things: a mind-boggling list of suggestions began to form on my notepad, each with a dainty "1 vote" written next to it. There were two things many votes had in common, however: you wanted lamb, and you wanted the curry to be BASTARD HOT. This is doable, I said, until I realized that to make a lamb curry that's good involves way too much slow cooking and probably overnight marinating. It wouldn't work. I needed depth of flavor, fast. That's basically the premise of the book, after all.

You will find in chapter 7 a recipe for really good lamb chops, which I hope will satisfy the lamb cravings, but they do require a little forward planning. In the meantime, the answer to the problem of late-night curry is seafood. Prawns, to be precise, and the easiest curry sauce in the world.

I've been making this recipe for ages, and I can confidently say that it is one of the best recipes for the drunken cook, ever. You don't even need to chop the onion—you just whack it in the blender with a few other things! It involves hardly any work, and the result is truly satisfying, incredible given the short (for a curry) list of ingredients. It's also quite healthy. Well, at least, it was until I started adding ghee to it. You could substitute oil if you like, and reduce the quantity, if healthy eating is your thing. I have to say, though, you're a strange kind of drunk. Personally, I'm all about the ghee, and obviously it gives the best, richest flavor to the finished dish. So use the ghee, basically.

Very Tasty Prawn Curry

1 large onion

5 cloves of garlic

1 in (2.5 cm) cube fresh ginger

3 fresh red chilies

2 tbsp ghee (or oil if you prefer. Wimp)

1 cinnamon stick

6 cardamom pods, crushed lightly so the pods crack open

2 tsp ground cumin

½ tsp ground coriander

14 oz (400 g) can chopped tomatoes

1 tbsp tomato paste

1 generous tbsp spiced (it needs to be spiced) mango chutney (I like Geeta's)

½ tsp ground turmeric

18 oz (500 g) king prawns

5 tbsp natural yogurt

Fresh cilantro (coriander)

Salt and freshly ground black pepper

Plain basmatic rice, naan bread, or whatever you like, to serve

Makes 4 servings with rice

1 Put the onion, garlic, ginger, and chilies in a blender or food processor with 3 tbsp water and blend to a paste.

2 Heat the ghee or oil in a large frying pan and add the cinnamon stick and cardamom pods. Stir for 1 minute, then add the onion paste. Cook, stirring, for about 5 minutes, until the liquid has evaporated. Add the cumin and coriander and cook, stirring, for 1 minute.

3 Add the chopped tomatoes (save the empty can) and tomato paste. Stir and keep cooking until all the liquid is gone and you are left with a sort of paste in the pan (about 10 minutes).

4 Fill the empty tomato can three-quarters full with water and add to the pan, along with the mango chutney and turmeric. Simmer for 10–15 minutes, until the sauce is thickened.

5 Get the rice going now, if you're having it.

6 Taste the curry sauce and season well with salt and pepper. Take the pan off the heat and add the prawns. Stir, then add the yogurt in two batches, stirring well each time. Put the pan back on the heat and simmer for a few minutes, until the prawns are heated through. Serve sprinkled with the fresh cilantro.

Dodging ... The Botulism Burger

The kind of food the drunken palate craves tends to lean toward what I term affectionately "a bit of filth." What I mean by that is of course not "dirty" in the biological, germy sense, but in the slightly over the top, naughty but nice sense. The drunken kitchen is the playground of the guilty pleasure. This is not a time for subtlety. I present to you, then, a burger that is high-quality, in the sense that you've made it yourself with (I hope) good ingredients, but it still retains a little shame, mostly by way of the excellent sauce. This recipe is by my friend Dan Vaux-Nobes, who writes the food blog Essex Eating. It's based on an American "fry sauce," basically a burger sauce (duh) with more than a touch of the Big Mac "special" sauce about it, but a bit more swagger. It is, basically, the best burger sauce recipe of all time. In your face, Ronald McDonald!

I've also used the "cloche method" to finish the burger, which involves returning the finished thing to the pan, splashing in a bit of water, and covering it briefly to allow it to steam inside. This doesn't just produce the shiniest, most appealing burger in the entire world, it also makes the whole thing a big juicy amalgam of meat, sauce, cheese, and softened garnish that will have juices running down your arms. You'll see fingers scooping at the plate to gather every last morsel and then realize that they are yours. Don't look back.

It is important that you get the buns toasted before you start making the burger, FYI, and that you have a lid ready to cover the pan before you start cooking. Basically, just read through the recipe first so you have everything ready to go. This is drunken cooking top tip number 2, remember.

Really Good Bad Burger

For Dan's Fry Sauce

1 tbsp French's classic yellow mustard

1½ tbsp tomato ketchup

2 heaped tbsp mayonnaise

1 tsp English mustard

2 heaped tbsp finely chopped gherkins or cornichons

2 dashes of Tabasco sauce

A dash of Worcester sauce

Freshly ground black pepper

For the burger

12½ oz (350 g) ground (minced) rump steak

2 slices processed cheese (or whatever cheese you prefer)

2 seeded burger buns, lightly toasted

Iceberg lettuce, shredded

Sweet gherkin pickles, sliced

Onion, thinly sliced

Salt and freshly ground black pepper

Makes 2 burgers

1 Make the sauce by mixing all the ingredients together. Set aside.

2 Divide the meat into two balls, then press into burger patties. Preheat a cast-iron skillet, griddle pan, or other heavy pan to a high heat.

3 Season the outside of the patties thoroughly with salt and pepper and slap into the pan. Cook for about 4 minutes each side for a medium burger. You don't need to oil the pan, but don't attempt to flip the burger before the 4 minutes is up, or it will stick.

4 Once flipped, put a slice of cheese on top of each burger while the underside cooks.

5 Place the burgers on one half of each bun, top with sauce, lettuce, pickles, onion, and the other bun half, and return to the pan immediately. Splash in a couple of tablespoons of water and immediately cover with a lid. Allow to steam for a minute or so, then remove to a plate and serve immediately.

CHAPTER 4

Cooking with Booze

A Dash of Booze

I want to celebrate all the different ways that booze can be used to maximize culinary success, and obviously, using it as an ingredient is one of them. The booze here is in the recipes and not necessarily in you, although don't let me lay down the law—it's your kitchen. I've still adhered to the rules of drunken cooking just in case, which means that the following recipes are all very easy to put together and also generally quite unhealthy. I make no apologies whatsoever for the latter.

Welsh Rarebit Crumpets

Always consider crumpets in place of bread. Think about it: all those holes soak up the eggy boozy mixture beautifully. It's a no-brainer. I make eggy bread in the same way. Once you've bitten into a booze-laced cheesy beer sponge you won't be looking back, trust me. Mmmm, boozy crumps.

1¾ oz (50 g) butter

1¾ oz (50 g) all-purpose (plain) flour

3 fl oz (80 ml) stout or other dark beer

7 oz (200 g) cheddar cheese, grated, or half and half cheddar and Lancashire, if you can find it

1 egg yolk

1½ tsp English mustard

1 scant tsp wholegrain mustard

A splash of Worcestershire sauce

8 crumpets (decent ones; cheaper brands are too thin)

Freshly ground black pepper

Makes 4 servings

1 In a pan, melt the butter and add the flour. Cook over a low heat for about 30 seconds, stirring constantly. Pour in the stout, slowly, stirring all the time.

2 Add the cheese, egg yolk, mustards, and Worcestershire sauce and cook until the cheese is melted, stirring constantly. Season with pepper and set the mixture aside to cool a little.

3 Toast the crumpets, making sure they are good and crisp, then spread them thickly with the cheese mixture. Put under a hot broiler (grill) until golden and bubbling. Now try to wait for them to cool down slightly before eating.

4 Any leftover mixture can be refrigerated and will be dangerously easy to pile high on toast or crumpets once thoroughly chilled. Just make sure you heat it through more slowly if cooking it straight from the fridge.

Mussels Cooked in Beer

Mussels bloody LOVE booze. Thirsty buggers. They need to be steamed open by the addition of liquid to the pan, so why not make that liquid as interesting as possible? Wine is often used, but some of the newer, craft beers are better. You want a beer that's hoppy but not crazily so, one with a good floral backbone. My favorite is Jaipur, but I think Goose Island IPA or Brewdog's Punk IPA also work well. Use whatever you like. You could use cider too, come to think of it, or any aniseed-flavored spirit, like Pernod, Ricard, or ouzo (scale back the quantity on those. Yikes!). I've included bacon, but—at risk of stating the obvious—leave it out for a pescatarian dish.

2¼ lb (1 kg) fresh mussels

2 tbsp oil

4 slices thick-cut smoked bacon, diced

1 white onion, finely chopped

1 celery stick, finely chopped

1 big clove of garlic, crushed

11 fl oz (330 ml) beer or other liquor (see above)

A small handful of fresh parsley, roughly chopped

Freshly ground black pepper

Lemon wedges and crusty bread, to serve

Makes 2 servings

1 Put the mussels into a colander and scrub them under cold running water, knocking off any barnacles and removing the gritty beards by giving them a sharp tug. Discard any mussels that do not close when you give them a sharp tap on the side of the sink. Also discard any that have broken shells.

2 Heat the oil in a pan large enough to hold the mussels. Add the bacon, onion, celery, and garlic and cook, stirring, until the bacon fat is beginning to crisp up.

3 Add the liquor and some black pepper and bring to the boil, then add the mussels. Put the lid on and cook on a medium-high heat for about 5 minutes, giving the pan a shake now and then, until the mussels have steamed open. Discard any mussels that don't open.

4 Divide between bowls, sprinkle with parsley and serve with the lemon wedges and bread.

Prawns Saganaki

When I asked my chef friend if he had any tips for making saganaki, he was all like "'Saganaki' just means 'pan,' doofus. So you want a recipe for a pan?" Sarcastic, yes, but a great friend and a brilliant chef who makes a mean version of this dish. It's Greek, the name of that pan, and there are many different ingredients that can be cooked in it. Most common, however, are seafood or cheese. The latter is often served "flaming," with ouzo or other booze poured over the pan-fried cheese, then set alight at the table. You can see why I thought it best to avoid that version here. Prawns, on the other hand, are fair game. They are safe. Reliable. Tasty. You also get cheese anyway, in the form of feta, so no complaining. In my opinion, it's one of the few recipes where seafood and cheese actually work well together.

4 tbsp olive oil

1 onion, diced

2 cloves of garlic, crushed

2 red chilies, finely chopped

3 tbsp ouzo (or another aniseed-flavored spirit)

14 oz (400 g) can good-quality chopped tomatoes

1 tbsp tomato paste

A pinch of superfine (caster) sugar

10½ oz (300 g) raw king prawns

5 oz (150 g) feta cheese

A good handful of fresh parsley leaves, chopped

Salt and freshly ground black pepper

Crusty bread or toasted pita, to serve

Makes 2 servings

1 In a frying pan that can go underneath the broiler (grill) (i.e. one that doesn't have a plastic handle), heat the olive oil and gently cook the onion until soft but not colored.

2 Add the garlic and chili and cook for a few minutes longer, then add the ouzo, tomatoes, tomato paste, sugar, and salt and pepper. Cook for 10 minutes or until thickened.

3 Stir in the prawns and dot the feta cheese on top of the sauce. Place under a medium broiler (grill) for about 10 minutes, or until the cheese is starting to color in places.

4 Sprinkle with the parsley and serve immediately, with bread.

Tartiflette

I recently mocked someone for saying that tartiflette is "the greatest dish in the world." I was all like "Really? The greatest dish in the world?!" but now I come to think of it, all the signs are there. It has bacon, which everyone knows is surely included in the Greatest Dish in the World. It contains potatoes, so there's an element of stodge, and it has loads of pungent yet creamy Reblochon cheese, a soft, washed-rind number from the French Alps, which is an excellent argument against pasteurization. (Sadly, due to the lack of pasteurization, it can be a little tricky to source genuine Reblochon in the US. Try the pasteurized Delice de Jura as an alternative; or Epoisses—it's aged a little longer than Reblochon but still uses raw milk, thereby neatly dodging the government killjoys.) There's wine, of course. Oh, and butter. Also, it's baked and so turns all gooey inside and crisp on top. It tastes, to be fair, like a strong contender for the title.

2¼ lb (1 kg) waxy potatoes

1 tbsp flavorless oil, for frying

1 onion, chopped

7 oz (200 g) bacon lardons

3¼ fl oz (100 ml) white wine

10 fl oz (300 ml) crème fraîche

1 lb (500 g) Reblochon cheese, sliced

Butter, for greasing

Salt and freshly ground black pepper

Cornichons and wine, to serve

Makes 6 servings

1 Preheat the oven to 375°F (190°C/Gas 5). Parboil the potatoes in a pan of boiling salted water until just tender, then drain and set aside to cool slightly.

2 Heat the oil in a frying pan on a pretty high heat, fry the onion and bacon for 10 minutes, or until golden brown, then splash in the white wine. Continue to cook until most of the liquid has evaporated.

3 Grease a 9 x 9 x 2 in. (23 x 23 x 5 cm) dish liberally with butter. Slice the potatoes, then put a layer in the dish, followed by a little crème fraîche, some of the bacon mixture, and a few slices of cheese. Season with salt and pepper, then repeat with the rest of the layers. Finish with a layer of cheese.

4 Stick it in the oven for 30 minutes, then whack it under a preheated broiler (grill) for 5 minutes or so, to crisp up the top.

Run Out of Wine?

No white wine in the house? No problem; use that old bottle of vermouth instead. When cooking anything with garlic, herbs, onions, or seafood, for example, whack in a slug of vermouth for a more aromatic finish. Just don't use it in the tartiflette.

Buttered Rum Sundae

Buttered rum is one of the greatest drinks of all time, particularly when it's raining outside, or snowing, or stormy, or just a bit chilly, or even quite warm really. Here I've made it into a sauce to use on the classiest of all desserts, the ice cream sundae. What? Oh come on, eat this and tell me you don't enjoy every mouthful. IT HAS BUTTER AND BOOZE IN IT.

For the buttered rum sauce

4¼ oz (120 g) muscovado (dark brown) sugar

4¼ oz (120 g) butter

5½ fl oz (160 ml) heavy (double) cream

3¼ fl oz (100 ml) rum

A very small pinch of ground cinnamon (optional—personally I can't stand the stuff)

For the sundae

Vanilla choc chip ice cream

Rum and raisin ice cream

Chopped nuts of your choice

Bittersweet (dark) chocolate, for grating

Makes 2–4 servings

To make the buttered rum sauce

1 Heat all the ingredients for the sauce together in a pan over a medium heat, stirring. When the mixture comes to the boil, let it cook for a few minutes until it thickens slightly. Allow to cool until just warm before using.

To make the sundae

1 Once the sauce has cooled slightly, fill a sundae glass with alternating scoops of the two ice cream flavors, sprinkling in nuts as you go.

2 Pour over more sauce than is decent and grate some of the chocolate on top.

New Orleans Bread Pudding with Whiskey Sauce

This is similar to a British bread-and-butter pudding, but contains practically no butter (don't panic, British people! It has other things going for it, I promise), and is served with a sauce flavored with whiskey (you see!). It satisfies any kind of sugar and carb cravings that might be going on. For this reason, this dish is suitable for other scenarios in this book, too (see Chapter 8: Hangovers).

1 lb (450 g) loaf of bread

2 pints (950 ml) milk

3 eggs, lightly beaten

7 oz (200 g) light brown sugar

1 tsp vanilla extract

¼ tsp ground allspice

A very small pinch of ground cinnamon, or to taste

3½ oz (100 g) raisins, golden if possible

3 tbsp butter, at room temperature, for greasing

For the whiskey sauce

4¼ oz (120 g) muscovado (dark brown) sugar

4¼ oz (120 g) butter

5½ fl. oz (160 ml) heavy (double) cream

3¼ fl. oz (100 ml) whiskey

Makes 8–10 servings

1 Preheat the oven to 350°F (180°C/ Gas 4). Cut the bread into cubes and place in a bowl. Add all the other pudding ingredients except the butter and leave to soak for 2 hours.

2 Grease an 11 x 8½ x 2 in (28 x 22 x 6 cm) dish with butter (or, you know, a dish roughly that size, it isn't going to matter). Tip the mixture into it and bake for 1 hour 30 minutes, or until golden and pulling away from the edges of the pan. Check it after an hour.

3 To make the sauce, heat all the ingredients together in a pan over a medium heat, stirring. Bring to the boil and cook for a few minutes until it thickens slightly. Allow to cool until just warm before using.

CHAPTER 5

The Perfect Pub

Pubs Not Bars

This chapter is about the British boozer (that's a pub, US readers). A place Brits go to get drunk, to read the paper, or to eat crisps and have a "swift half," which translates as eating crisps and drinking five pints. The reason pubs are so much better than bars is they are steeped (literally) in history. They are cozy dens of debauchery without the sterility, cleanliness, or lack of personality of many bars. They come at the end of a long walk on a sunny day, preferably along the coast. Either that, or they are a "local," the hub of the community, in which the floor is coated with your own blood, sweat and tears.

The eternal search

I have never managed to find the perfect pub. A couple of places have come close—neither of them near my home, annoyingly. Proximity of pub to front door is very important, and the "local" is cherished for many reasons: the sense of community (it's hard to beat that Cheers feeling when you walk in and immediately see familiar faces); the potential for "nipping out for a swift one" before lunch (famous last words); and the option, should one wish, to bed in before finally rolling home at 2am (it's fine, you're only five minutes away). Local pubs, however, tend to be forgiven many failings simply due to their location. They rarely fill more than a few criteria for the Perfect Pub, which, for me, are as follows:

1 The Perfect Pub needs to be a "proper boozer," by which I mean a proper British pub. It is not a faceless wine bar, the kind of place that serves food called something along the lines of—hold me—"British tapas" (vomits) and churns out endless bottles of watery white wine to people in suits. The perfect pub is cozy, with an independent feel. It has regular customers, bubble pint glasses, comfortable seats, and a roaring log fire in the winter.

2 It must have a fine selection of booze. It's debatable whether the perfect pub serves both good beer and good wine. A solid spirits selection seems to go with both, but good beer and wine tend to remain in separate establishments. We do not have space here to get into the politics of breweries and landlords and the options (or lack of) available to each, but seriously, it cannot be too much to ask for a few solid beers and some well-chosen bottles.

3 There is a "pub cat."

4 No children. Sorry.

5 There is a jukebox. Maybe. If there is, it is free and it definitely does not contain any shit music.

6　People are not allowed to reserve tables. At the risk of sounding like an old woman, this is a problem with a lot of pubs nowadays. A pub should be a place where one can idly walk in of an afternoon or evening on the spur of the moment, sit down, and settle in. It should not be a place of frustration. Very often I have entered a pub with the aim of having a quiet pint, only to walk around for 10 minutes trying to find a table that hasn't been reserved for "Becky, from 2pm." It finally becomes apparent that the only genuinely "free" table in my own bloody local pub is the crappy one right by the door. At worst (and this has happened to me), every single one of the "free" tables is reserved, so you then have to leave a pub full of empty tables because some idiots don't know the function of a proper boozer. THE CRAPPY CHAINS WERE MADE FOR YOU PEOPLE. USE THEM!

7　Of course I am going to get to the food, but before I do may I please, please say that if a pub serves food it should be remembered that many people still want to come and "just drink." Just drink! In a pub! The outrage. So many pubs these days give the entire space over to tables for serving food and forget about nurturing the regulars who want a quiet pint and the newspaper.

8　And so to the food. The perfect pub obviously has great bar food, yet it is not a "gastropub," a term that was adopted by any pub fancying itself a bit whizzy in the kitchen. The perfect pub does not serve mediocre Thai food either, as has been common for many really bad pubs in the last ten years. I won't offer my theory here as to why that became a "thing," because it will almost certainly get me into trouble.

On the menu

For a start there will be the usual food on offer: a good selection of crisps (potato chips), which absolutely must include the classic flavors—salt and vinegar, cheese and onion, prawn cocktail, etc. I went to a pub recently where it was not possible to order a bag of crisps with a flavor that wasn't something along the lines of "lobster bisque and chili jam." No.

Nuts can do one, but I'm completely behind the stinkiest of all bar snacks, the scampi fry. Nothing, nothing, makes a person stink more than a packet of scampi fries. If you're really "lucky," a boozer might stock the Holy Trinity of scampi fries, bacon fries, and (shudder) cheese moments, the last being truly terrifying and certainly devoid of any cheese.

Pork scratchings are, of course, essential, even if only in their bought-in form. Some places make them, which is fine, but I must urge the publican to be careful on this front. Making a good pork scratching is an art, and there are rules that must be followed, not least that all hairs should be removed before frying. I speak as someone who once had a pig bristle from a pork scratching stuck in their throat for two weeks. It was eventually tweezed from my sedated throat by a doctor at the local hospital. I rest my case.

A final mention, before we move on, for the pickled egg, which I adore. People of (cough) a certain age will remember the fashion for dumping a pickled egg into a packet of crisps (chips), giving it a good shake and eating the remaining smush as a bar snack. I certainly do. I still do it on occasion, or at least I would if I could find a boozer that still served both pickled eggs and crisps.

Those are the salty snacks and nibbles out of the way, but what about the more substantial fare? Here are some recipes for the food I would like to see in my perfect pub.

The Ultimate Ploughman's

The ploughman's lunch, for me, is the perfect pub meal. It is elusive nowadays, and usually found only in country pubs. It is a good meal, come to think of it, for the pub that doesn't really "do" food, being as it is essentially an assembly job. It depends almost entirely on the quality of the ingredients, unless we're talking about the perfect pub, in which case they'd cook the ham and make the pickles themselves. I'm not suggesting you do that of course (unless you want to, firecracker!), but it's imperative that you buy the best of everything, and that you have the correct amounts of each, as follows:

1 There should be ham and cheese. So often the hungry drinker is forced to choose between the ham and the cheese ploughman's. Why?! Surely anyone in their right mind wants both? I know I bloody do. The ham should be honey-glazed and thickly sliced, its milky white fat studded with cloves. The cheese should be plentiful, and there should be more than one type. Three, in fact. A hard cheese like Lord of the

Hundreds would be nice, and then a really superb cheddar, obviously, all flinty and full of itself. Then a blue cheese like Stilton or Stichelton. Yes. That would do very nicely. A few slices of apple and some grapes work well alongside.

2 The pickles should be plentiful and varied. Pickles are an absolutely essential part of a ploughman's. First, there should be pickled onions, both the small, sweet silverskin ones and the "proper" malt-pickled, spiced ones with just the right balance of sweet and cat's-backside, face-puckering sour. I would then like some pickled red cabbage—an English pickle that gets overlooked for no fathomable reason, and then, finally, a good dollop of bright yellow piccalilli (preferably made by my mother, who makes the best piccalilli in the world). A piccalilli should be really quite tart, with a good hit of mustard and—essentially—very crisp vegetables. Since this is a fantasy world, in which I clearly have more than one stomach, why not throw a wedge of pork pie on the side?

3 The salad is so often a sad little afterthought. The base should be of English butter lettuce, which is one of the world's greatest lettuces, sadly pushed down the hierarchy in favor of impostors like the literally pointless and irritatingly frilly lollo rosso or everyone's favorite bully—arugula (rocket). Neither has any place on this very British plate. Scallions (spring onions) are essential, as is a bit of cucumber and tomato, although the latter only in summer. I'll take a few radishes if they're available.

4 Condiments. Salad cream is perfect for dipping those scallions into, and also for coating the large, soft, petal-like leaves of the butter lettuce. No other salad dressing is needed if the salad is present. Not for me. Mustard—both English and wholegrain—is essential for spreading on the ham. Oh, and Branston pickle should always make an appearance. I will not tolerate any of the horrible sweet chutneys or sugary tomato "jams" that seem to prevail nowadays. Why has no one noticed that they don't taste very nice?

5 Bread. This should come with an obscenely large wedge of good-quality salted butter. The bread may be white or wholewheat (preferably both are available), and should be well made and incredibly fresh. It should have some substance, a decent flavor, and a hardy crust. If it were slightly warm I'd be extremely happy. The best ploughman's always have bread served in wedges cut from circular loaves, so one ends up with a cake slice-shaped doorstop of bread from which to tear hunks. "Hunk" is the sort of word that should be used when eating a ploughman's.

Really Decent Steak Sandwich

Ahh, the steak sandwich, a pub classic! It is so often served so badly. I think the poor state of steak sandwiches in pubs is second only to those on hotel room-service menus. The steak is always overcooked, each slice a little rubbery tongue, impossible to bite into but excellent at pulling out all the other fillings with it. Each bite necessitates the emergency "grab and pull from the mouth with fingers" technique that is oh-so-bloody desirable when eating. The condiments never have enough punch, the bread is never properly considered, and don't even get me started on the tepid temperature.

People make the mistake of thinking sandwiches are very easy to make well, which is, frankly, bullshit. Attention to detail is very important. What follows is a recipe for a really decent steak sandwich. The rump steak has plenty of flavor and, crucially, ends up with a texture that actually works in a sandwich. It goes without saying that one should buy the best quality available. Mayonnaise should be homemade if at all possible, for the sake of attention to detail again; homemade mayo is just far superior to the store-bought stuff. I like two types of mustard—English for heat and wholegrain for tartness—and the peppery backbone of watercress. The quick pickled onions add bites of sweet'n'sour allium twang, and are good with lots of meat dishes, actually, whenever a bit of acidity is needed.

For the quick pickled onions

½ pint (250 ml) cider vinegar or good-quality white wine vinegar

2½ tbsp superfine (caster) sugar

3 tsp salt

2 red onions, halved and thinly sliced

For the mayonnaise

2 egg yolks

Oil (ideally vegetable or groundnut/peanut; don't use olive oil, whether extra-virgin or otherwise)

Juice of ½–1 lemon

Salt and freshly ground black pepper

To make the onions

1 Make the onions an hour before you want to make the sandwich. (You should also take the steak out of the fridge at this point.) Combine the vinegar, sugar, and salt until the sugar and salt have dissolved.

2 Place the onions in a jar and pour the pickling mixture over. Seal and leave at room temperature for an hour. This recipe makes a lot, but they will keep in the fridge in their jar for several weeks.

To make the mayonnaise

1 Put the egg yolks in a clean bowl and whisk them together. (You'll find this easiest with an electric whisk.) Whisk in the oil a few drops at a time, making sure each bit is fully incorporated before adding the next.

2 As you whisk in more oil and the mayo starts to thicken, you can start adding the oil in very slightly larger quantities until you are steadily adding a thin stream. Stop adding the oil when the mayo is slightly thicker than you want it to be, then whisk in the lemon juice. Check the seasoning and add more salt and pepper if necessary.

3 The key with mayo is to be cautious with the oil until you get a feel for making it. If you add too much at once, it will "split" or curdle. If this happens, don't despair. Put a fresh egg yolk in a clean bowl and begin adding the split mixture to it, very slowly, just as if it were the oil. This should bring it back.

12½ oz (350 g) rump steak

2 sourdough rolls, a sourdough baguette, or other bread with some backbone

2 fat cloves of garlic

English or Dijon mustard, to taste

Wholegrain mustard, to taste

A handful of watercress, roughly chopped

Salt and freshly ground black pepper

Makes 2 sandwiches

To make the sandwich

1 To cook the steak, get the pan very hot but do not add any oil. Season the meat—it's now at room temperature, remember?—very generously on both sides just before cooking. Add more salt and pepper than you think is right.

2 You will need to turn the steak regularly, say every minute. This is the best method for ensuring a well-cooked steak with a great crust outside and juicy meat within; 3 minutes in total on each side should do it. Set the steak aside in a warm place to rest for 5–10 minutes.

3 Toast the bread. Cut the garlic cloves in half and rub them aggressively all over the toasted sides of the bread while it is still warm. Spread mayonnaise on one side of the bread, followed by a little English or Dijon mustard on the other side, and then a slick of wholegrain mustard.

4 Slice the steak and add it to the sandwiches, followed by some pickled onions and watercress. Serve immediately.

Prawn Cocktail

Prawn cocktail is a brilliant dish. I will stand by that statement. Yes, it became unfashionable, but I'm not bothered about what is fashionable and what isn't. It tastes great, and it is even better when loaded onto prawn cocktail crisps (potato chips). What? Go on, try it. I dare you. Serve in a bubble pint glass for maximum pubby-ness.

2 tbsp mayonnaise

1 tbsp tomato ketchup

Tabasco sauce, to taste

A small squeeze of lemon juice, plus 2 lemon wedges

7 oz (200 g) cooked shrimp (prawns)

2 iceberg lettuce leaves, shredded, plus extra whole leaves for lining the dishes

½ avocado, peeled and diced

1 scallion (spring onion), finely chopped

Cayenne pepper

Salt and freshly ground black pepper

Prawn cocktail crisps (chips), to serve

Makes 2 servings

1 Mix the mayonnaise, tomato ketchup, Tabasco, a conservative squeeze of lemon juice (you can add more later), and some salt and pepper. Stir in the shrimp (prawns). Mix together the shredded lettuce, avocado, and scallion (spring onion).

2 Line the serving dishes with the whole lettuce leaves (don't skip this, because it adds a lovely crunch), then put the shredded lettuce mix inside.

3 Top with shrimp, sprinkle with cayenne and serve with a lemon wedge and the prawn cocktail crisps.

Pork Pie

I'm not going to lie to you—this is a two-day job and it takes a while. You know what I'm going to say, though, don't you? Uh-huh. It's worth it. Also, it's going to last you and your perfect pub for ages, depending how many people you let through the door, of course. A wedge of homemade pork pie and a dollop of piccalilli should be on the menu, without a shadow of a doubt.

This recipe makes one absolute beast of a pie, which fills an 9½ in (23.5 cm) cake pan. Start making the pie the day before you want to eat it.

For the stock

A few pork bones

1 pig's trotter

1 onion, halved and studded with six cloves

1 celery stick, halved

6 black peppercorns

Parsley stalks

2 bay leaves

About 4¼ pints (2 liters) water

For the crust

3½ oz (100 g) butter

3½ oz (100 g) lard

6¾ fl oz (200 ml) water

1¼ lb (550 g) all-purpose plain flour

1½ tsp salt

2 large eggs, plus another for glazing later

1 bay leaf

To make the stock

1 Put all the ingredients for the stock in a pan and simmer gently for 3–4 hours, skimming off any scum as necessary. Strain, then leave in the fridge overnight or until well chilled and set to a jelly.

2 Scrape the layer of fat off the top, and the stock is ready to be reheated. You will need about 8½ fl oz (250 ml) for the pie (don't try to get any more in, trust me). The rest is a very valuable addition to your freezer.

To make the crust

1 Melt the butter and lard with the water over a gentle heat. Mix the flour and salt in a large bowl, then add the 2 eggs. Use a knife to start cutting the mixture together.

For the filling

2¾ lb (1.3 kg) pork shoulder

8½ oz (250 g) smoked back bacon

8½ oz (250 g) belly pork, ground (minced)

1 heaped tbsp chopped fresh sage

1 tbsp chopped fresh thyme leaves

1 heaped tsp salt

1 heaped tsp freshly ground black pepper, or to taste

1 heaped tsp white pepper, or to taste

½ tsp ground mace

Makes 8–10 servings

2 Begin adding the melted fat and water mixture a little at a time until everything starts to come together, then use your hands to bring it into a ball shape.

3 Knead very briefly until smooth, then wrap in plastic wrap and refrigerate while you make the filling.

To make the filling

1 Dice the pork shoulder, removing any sinewy bits. Finely dice the bacon and mix all three meats together. Add the rest of the ingredients and combine well.

2 Take a little of the mixture and form into a small patty about the size of a cucumber slice, then cook in a frying pan to check the seasoning and adjust to taste as necessary.

To make the pie

1 Preheat the oven to 350°F (180°C/Gas 4). Cut off a third of the pastry and set aside for the lid (put it back in the fridge), then roll out the remaining two-thirds on a lightly floured surface. You want a circle big enough to cover the base and sides of your cake pan, which you need to grease with butter.

2 Mold the pastry into the pan, making sure there are no gaps, then stuff with the filling. It will shrink during cooking, leaving room for the jelly.

3 Roll out the remaining pastry to make the lid, and brush the edges of the pie with beaten egg before putting the lid on top and crimping and sealing well with your fingers.

4 Make a hole in the top of the pie and bake in the center of the oven for half an hour. Reduce the heat to 320°F (160°C/Gas 2) and bake for another hour, then remove the pie from the pan and brush all over with beaten egg before baking it for another 10–15 minutes.

5 Leave the pie to cool for half an hour, then reheat 8½ fl oz (250 ml) stock until it is just liquid enough to pour into the pie. Funnel it in very slowly through the hole in the top.

6 Allow the pie to cool completely and chill it to allow the jelly to set completely. The pie is lovely with piccalilli and a pale ale.

Roast Potatoes, Gravy, and Cheese

I've sort of pinched this idea from the Canadians, as they do something similar, called "poutine." It's their junk food, really, and involves topping fries with cheese curds and gravy. This is a British take on the idea, based on the tales I've heard from (ahem) slightly older people who wistfully recall the days when roast potatoes would be left on the bar in the pub at the end of Sunday lunch service, for customers to help themselves before they got kicked out for the afternoon. That's right, whippersnappers, pubs used to close in the afternoon! Unthinkable.

1¾ oz (50 g) goose fat or lard

1 lb (500 g) Maris Piper or Desirée (or other floury) potatoes

1 tbsp oil

1 tbsp Marmite or other yeast extract

Gravy (store-bought, or homemade if you're very enthusiastic)

Your choice of cheese (I use whatever melting cheese I have available, or a mixture)

Salt

Makes 3–4 servings

1 Preheat the oven to 375°F (190°C/Gas 5). Put the fat in a small roasting pan (tray) and heat it in the oven while you prepare the potatoes.

2 Peel and cut the potatoes into evenly sized pieces. Rinse them under cold running water for a few minutes to get rid of excess starch. Place them in a large pan and cover with cold water. Season with salt, bring to the boil, and parboil for 10 minutes.

3 Drain the potatoes and leave them in the colander to steam dry for a few minutes. Don't skip this step. After that time, give the colander a shake so that the edges of the potatoes get really roughed up—those are your crispy bits.

4 Mix the oil and Marmite in a small bowl, pour over the potatoes and mix to coat evenly.

5 Carefully remove the hot pan from the oven and place the potatoes in it, spooning the fat over the potatoes to make sure they are all completely covered. Roast for about an hour, or until golden brown all over. They won't need turning.

6 Once cooked, pour over the gravy and dot with pieces of cheese. Sling under a medium broiler (grill) until the cheese melts.

CHAPTER 6

Mates

Party Time

There are two potential scenarios here. The first is that you've all been out to a bar or the pub, and you've instigated the "Let's all go back to mine! Wahey!" scenario (followed closely by the "Shit, when was the last time I washed the dishes?" scenario). "So much cheaper than eating out! So much more fun! Let's cook!" You've not been as organized as the Do Ahead Drunk (see Chapter 7), but you still need something reliable that is easy to make in bulk and is guaranteed to sledgehammer around the drunken palate with the subtlety of a rabid dog. The second is the situation in which you've planned to have people over, but haven't been terribly organized and/or you've gotten overexcited and started ploughing into the wine at around 12.30, then rapidly lost the will to cook, and/or you just want to spend time with people rather than scurrying back and forth in the kitchen like an anxious whippet.

Obscenely Large Garlic Butter Loaf, with Cheese or 'Nduja

This is essentially a way of making cheesy garlic bread for a shitload of people at once. I can also see this pull-apart behemoth deployed with a hangover, to be picked at from the comfort of the sofa, pre- and post-snooze. There are many embellishments that can be added to the basic garlic butter, but I must say I do enjoy the classic hookup between cheese and onion. Still, I give some suggestions below. There are many options. My favorite is to omit the cheese and onion and add blobs of 'nduja, a spicy Calabrian sausage that melts into scarlet red pools and soaks into the bread.

1 sourdough loaf, unsliced

12½ oz (350 g) cheddar cheese, grated

5 oz (150 g) butter

2 or 3 cloves of garlic, crushed (personally I love garlic, so often add more, but just adapt to your taste— this ain't highfalutin)

4 scallions (spring onions), finely shredded

A handful of fresh parsley leaves, finely chopped

Makes 6–8 servings

1 Variations and suggestions for embellishments: chili flakes, pine nuts, chipotle flakes, bacon bits, very ripe diced tomatoes, za'atar, Parmesan cheese, pesto, mozzarella, mustard, crumbled sausage, 'nduja, smoked garlic, rosemary, oregano.

2 Preheat the oven to 325°F (170°C/Gas 3). Cut the loaf in a crisscross pattern almost but not the whole way through. Put on a baking sheet lined with foil, and stuff the grated cheese into the gaps.

3 Melt the butter with the garlic and cook gently for 2 minutes. Add the embellishments, then drizzle over the cut loaf. Sprinkle over the parsley and scallions (spring onions). Wrap in foil and bake for 15 minutes.

Pig Cheek Tacos with Blood Orange and Chipotle

Oil and flour, for searing the cheeks

10 pig cheeks

2 onions, finely chopped

2 carrots, very finely chopped

4 cloves

6 allspice berries

1 cinnamon stick

1 tbsp crushed chipotle chilies (or to taste)

Juice of 1 large blood orange

2 bay leaves

1 tbsp fresh oregano leaves

2 tbsp tomato paste

1 tsp sugar

2 pints (1 litre) vegetable stock (or enough to cover the cheeks comfortably; the sauce will be reduced at the end)

Salt and freshly ground black pepper

Soft tacos and guacamole, to serve

Makes 8 servings

I first published this recipe on my blog, Food Stories, in January 2011, and it is still by far one of the most popular recipes on the site. The combination of blood orange and chipotle is just indecently good. If you're going to leave a pot simmering on the hob, make sure you have it on the lowest heat possible, and, needless to say (yet again), make sure you're not away too long. A slow cooker would be a particularly safe option. If the thought of leaving it home alone is too much to bear, then may I remind you that it is definitely legal to drink alcohol in your own home. There is of course the possibility of making this dish when sober, too! I know—radical thinking.

To make the pig cheek tacos

1 Heat a few tablespoons of oil in a large, heavy pan. Dust some flour onto a plate and use it to coat the pig cheeks by turning them over on the plate. Once the oil is hot, sear the cheeks a few at a time until brown on all sides, then set aside on a plate.

2 Add the onions and carrots to the pan and cook for 5 minutes or so, until softened. Add the spices and chilies (in a little bit of muslin if you want to be fancy and make it easy to fish them out later on), orange juice, bay leaves, oregano, tomato paste, sugar, and stock, bring to the boil, then reduce to a simmer.

3 Put the pig cheeks back in the pan, put a lid on, and cook on the lowest heat possible for 3 hours. After this time, check the sauce for seasoning and add salt and pepper as necessary.

4 Remove the meat from the sauce; it should be extremely tender and falling apart at the touch. Shred it and set aside.

5 Fish the whole spices out of the sauce, then reduce it over a high heat by about two-thirds. Basically, you want enough to coat the meat in a rich sauce. Put the meat back in the sauce and warm through.

6 Serve on tacos with the pickled onions and guacamole. To make "tacos," use a large glass, teacup, or knife to cut circles from a large fajita wrap, and toast lightly in a dry pan.

For the pickled onions

2 red onions, sliced

5 fl oz (150 ml) orange juice

3 fl oz (80 ml) lime juice

1 tbsp sugar

1 tsp salt

To make the pickled onions

1 Place the onions in a bowl and cover with boiling water. Leave for 10 minutes, then drain. Mix the fruit juices together and stir in the sugar and salt until dissolved. Pour over the onions and leave for at least half an hour before eating.

Kind of Queso Fundido

This recipe would normally be made with Oaxacan cheese from Mexico. If you have trouble finding it, use the mixture of cheddar and mozzarella I've specified below to give a nice melting finish with decent punchy flavor. Don't be tempted to make it entirely with cheddar, as the mixture will split instead of melting together into a wondrous pot of goo—which is, obviously, what we're aiming for. It's like a spicy Mexican fondue, really.

5 oz (150 g) cooking chorizo, skinned and crumbled

1 onion, finely chopped

2 cloves of garlic

A pinch of ground cumin

2 fl oz (60 ml) tequila

Half a 14 oz (400 g) can good-quality chopped tomatoes

7 oz (200 g) Oaxaca cheese (or 4½ oz/125g mozzarella and 2½ oz/75 g cheddar), grated

A handful of cilantro (coriander) leaves

Salt and freshly ground black pepper

Tortilla chips or warm tortillas, to serve

Makes enough dip for a packet of tortilla chips

1 In a pan, cook the chorizo, moving it around until the oil starts to leach out. Add the onion, garlic, and cumin and cook until the onion is translucent. Season, then add the tequila and tomatoes and cook until you have a thick mixture.

2 Place the mixture in a heatproof dish, then sprinkle with the cheese and put under a hot broiler (grill) until the cheese is bubbling and melted.

3 Top with the cilantro (coriander) and serve with tortilla chips or warm tortillas.

Baked Buffalo Wings

We've outlawed deep-frying in this book, but that doesn't mean that anyone, ever, should be denied the joy of buffalo wings. I've cooked wings in just about every way possible, and these really are pretty damn good, despite lack of submersion in oil or meeting with BBQ grill. Hell, it's crisp chicken skin coated in melted butter and hot sauce. Come on! Also included is an optional blue cheese dip, if you're into that sort of thing.

Flour, for dredging

30 chicken wings (if you can, get your butcher to cut them into smaller pieces: tip, wingtip, and drumette)

8½ oz (250 g) butter

Chili sauce, to taste (Frank's original is the best sauce for the job, I find)

Salt and freshly ground black pepper

For the blue cheese dip

5 oz (150 g) blue cheese (I like Roquefort)

5 oz (150 g) natural yogurt

1 clove of garlic, crushed

1 tbsp lemon juice

1 tsp mustard (ideally Dijon)

1 tbsp chives, snipped with scissors

Makes 30 wings

To make the wings

1 Preheat the oven to 350°F (180°C/Gas 4). Spread a plate with flour and season it with salt and pepper. Dredge the wings in the seasoned flour, then bake for 25 minutes.

2 While they are baking, melt the butter and add chili sauce to taste. Mix well.

3 Remove the wings from the oven and coat them with half the sauce. Put them back in the oven for a further 5 minutes. Remove and toss with the rest of the sauce. Serve immediately.

To make the blue cheese dip

1 Mix all the dip ingredients together until combined, leaving the odd chunk of blue cheese in there, and chill.

Peckham Punch

Ice

1¼ pints (600 ml) dark rum

¾ pint (350 ml) Malibu

1¼ pints (600 ml) pineapple juice

1¼ pints (600 ml) orange juice

10 drops Angostura bitters

1¾ fl oz (50 ml) hibiscus syrup or grenadine

Juice of 10 limes

Orange slices

Pineapple slices

Makes 8–10 servings

No, that's not something you do in a fight. This is a Caribbean rum punch recipe, although I call it Peckham Punch because of the coconut and hibiscus flavors I use (both of which I really got to grips with when I moved to this vibrant area of southeast London). If you can't find hibiscus syrup, use the more traditional grenadine instead. Paper umbrellas and spectacles made out of drinking straws at the ready!

1 Put the ice in a large bowl and add all the other ingredients except the orange and pineapple slices.

2 Mix well, then use the fruit to decorate the bowl of punch.

Red Snapper

A red snapper is basically a Bloody Mary but better, because it does away with vodka and uses gin. I have never been a fan of vodka since a particular incident when … actually, you don't need to know. Gin, on the other hand, is one of the finest drinks in the entire world, so the substitution is a no-brainer.

A couple of pinches of celery salt

1¾ fl oz (50 ml) gin

About 10 fl oz (300 ml) tomato juice

2 dashes of Tabasco sauce, or to taste

3 dashes of Worcestershire sauce, or to taste

A squeeze of lemon juice

Ice

Makes 1 serving

1 Rim a glass with celery salt.

2 Shake all the other ingredients over ice, pour into the glass, and drink immediately.

3 Some people put celery sticks in their Bloody Mary or Snapper, but personally I think it just gets in the way.

CHAPTER 7

Do Ahead

Get Planning

There's a lot to be said for a bit of organization when it comes to getting the most out of sating the drunken appetite. There are, as ever, a couple of potential scenarios. The first is very gratifying, and it involves whacking something in the oven to cook low and slow, while you bugger off to the pub for a couple of pints, then return to a kitchen filled with the incredible smell of, say, slow-roasted lamb that is very nearly ready to eat. A little prep can be very rewarding. Just make sure you have only a couple of pints, yeah? No forgetting about the lamb and coming back at midnight to find a lump of charcoal in the oven and a major cleanup job on your hands.

The eternal search

The other kind of do-ahead drunk is all about the marinating. A ten-minute prep job in the morning or even the night before means you can be utterly smug the next day when you knock out something incredibly tasty in next to no time. I also have a personal agenda here, because this chapter allowed me to get some really decent spiced and/or slow-cooked recipes into this book. I always have to have everything my way, you see.

Beef Ragu with Gremolata

Olive oil, for frying

2 onions, finely diced

2 large celery sticks, lightly peeled and finely diced

2 large carrots, finely diced

2 bay leaves, slightly torn

2 large cloves of garlic, very finely chopped

1¾ lb (800 g) beef shin

14 oz (400 g) can chopped tomatoes

1 bottle red wine

A large sprig of fresh thyme, leaves only

Salt and freshly ground black pepper

Pasta, to serve

For the gremolata

A handful of fresh parsley leaves, very finely chopped

2 cloves of garlic, very finely chopped

Zest of 2 unwaxed lemons, finely chopped or grated (if you can only get waxed lemons, give them a good scrub under hot water)

Makes 4–6 servings

I've been cooking this dish for years, and it never fails to impress. Time is the magic ingredient. Well, that and the marrow that leaches out of the beef shin bones to enrich the sauce. The gremolata is magic finishing dust for your ragu; it's a zippy, enthusiastic puppy in comparison to the wise, shaggy, rich old hound that is the stew. Okay, I'm talking bollocks. But it makes the ragu taste better, so don't leave it out.

To make the ragu

1 Put some olive oil in a large, heavy pan, add the onions, celery, carrots, bay leaves, and garlic, and sweat gently, with the lid on, for 10–15 minutes, until softened.

2 Season the beef shin well all over and add it and the rest of the ingredients (except the pasta) to the pan. Bring to the boil, then turn down very low, put the lid on, and simmer gently for 3–4 hours, until the sauce is thick and the meat is falling off the bone.

3 Remove and discard all the pieces of bone. Flake the meat if it hasn't done so by itself, and put it back in the sauce. Adjust the seasoning and serve mixed through pasta of your choice (pappardelle are good, as they are big and robust).

To make the gremolata

1 Just mix everything together. Sprinkle it over your finished pasta.

Peshawar Lamb Chops

So you're having mates over tomorrow and you want the opportunity to sink a few and have a laugh without spending all your time mucking about in the kitchen. It's not sociable and it's not really that fun if you've been cooking for so long that you can't be bothered even to eat the meal at the end of it. I think we've all been there. I'll start, then, with a recipe for Pakistani spiced lamb chops. Get the marinade

together the day before, wang them all in the fridge overnight, and the meat will need only very quick cooking the next day.

There is a restaurant in east London called Tayyabs, which is famous for its lamb chops. They are smothered in an intensely spiced marinade then grilled for a really smoky flavor. They're so addictive that every last morsel of spice must be sucked from the bones, and, of course, the chef keeps the recipe a secret. I've had a go at replicating it here. Serve the chops piled high with a lot of napkins, or, if you really want to be practical about it, a whole kitchen roll per person. You'll see. The yogurt sauce makes for a very nice bit of dippy dippy on the side as you feast, medieval banquet-style, on a big ol' plate of chops. Throw the bones over your shoulder once you've gnawed them clean, for maximum jinks. Drinking from a goblet would be a nice touch, come to think of it. This recipe can easily be scaled up to feed more people.

10 small lamb chops

6 cloves of garlic, crushed

2 in (5 cm) piece of fresh ginger, grated

1½ tsp salt

1 tsp chili powder

1 tsp turmeric

1 tsp ground coriander

1 tsp ground cumin

½ tsp ground cinnamon

2 tsp garam masala

Juice of ½ lemon

3½ oz (100 g) thick yogurt

1 tsp freshly ground black pepper

Melted butter or ghee, for brushing

For the raita

4 tbsp natural yogurt

A small handful of fresh mint leaves, finely shredded

Juice of ½ lime

Salt and freshly ground black pepper

Makes 10 chops

To make the lamb chops

1 Place each chop between two pieces of plastic wrap and bash out with a meat mallet or rolling pin until roughly half the thickness.

2 Mix all the remaining ingredients except the butter or ghee and pour onto the chops, really working it into the meat. Cover and refrigerate for at least 8 hours, preferably overnight. I've marinated them for 48 hours before with incredible results, but it depends just how much of a do-ahead drunk you can be.

3 Heat a griddle pan to a very high heat and cook the chops for a couple of minutes on each side (or use a BBQ grill or broiler/grill if you prefer).

To make the raita

1 Beat the yogurt with a fork until smooth. Add the mint and lime juice, and some salt and pepper. You can also make this the day before; just give it a good stir and allow to warm up a little before serving.

Frying Pan Pizza

Yuh-huh. You're probably thinking I wouldn't faff about making my own pizza. Well, you're wrong. This is really fun to cook and it is actually the only way you can make decent pizza in your own home. The frying-pan method works because it gets enough heat on the base; domestic ovens don't get anywhere near hot enough to cook a pizza properly.

This recipe comes from the Pizza Pilgrims, brothers James and Thom Elliot, who quit their "proper jobs" to take a pizza pilgrimage around Italy. They now make sublime Neapolitan pizzas for lucky Londoners. You can read their story at pizzapilgrims.co.uk. You will need a large, non-stick frying pan for this recipe. I use a cast-iron skillet.

2¼ lb (1 kg) '00' flour with a high gluten content (such as Caputo Blue "Pizzeria")

2g fresh baker's yeast

1¼ pints (600 ml) cold water

1 oz (30 g) table salt

For the tomato sauce and toppings

14 oz (400 g) can good-quality Italian plum tomatoes, blitzed briefly and seasoned

A good pinch of sea salt

Grated Parmesan cheese

A handful of fresh basil leaves

5 oz (150 g) fior di latte (cow's-milk mozzarella), torn into pieces no bigger than a slice of cucumber

Extra-virgin olive oil, for drizzling

Makes 8 pizzas

To make the pizza dough

1 Tip the flour onto a clean work surface and make a well in the center. Dissolve the yeast in the water and pour into the well a little at a time, while using your hands to bring the walls of the flour in so that the water begins to thicken.

2 Once the mixture has reached the consistency of custard, add the salt and bring in the rest of the flour until it comes together as a dough. Knead for 10–15 minutes.

3 Cover and leave to rest for 10 minutes before kneading again quickly for 10 seconds (this helps to develop the flavor and the gluten).

4 Divide the dough into balls roughly 7 oz (200 g) in size and leave to rest overnight or for at least 8 hours (24 hours is best, 48 hours maximum) in a sealed container or a deep baking dish sprinkled with flour and covered in plastic wrap.

To make the pizza

1 Place a proved dough ball on a well-floured surface. Using your fingertips, press the dough ball out firmly, starting at the center and working out toward the edge. Ensure that you leave about ½ in (1 cm) around the rim of the pizza "unpressed" to create a crust. Turn the dough over and repeat this process on the other side, using more flour if needed.

2 Take the flattened dough on the back of your hands, resting on your knuckles. Pull your hands apart to stretch the dough out as far as you can without tearing it. Turn the dough through 90 degrees and repeat this stretching. Do this a few times, until you have a consistently thin piece of dough with a thicker rim. Now we are ready to cook.

3 Preheat the broiler (grill) to its highest setting and preheat a frying pan on a high heat. When it is very hot, lay the pizza base flat in it (do not use any oil).

4 Spread a thin layer of the blitzed plum tomatoes over the base, leaving about 1 in. (2.5 cm) round the edge for the crust. Add a pinch of Parmesan, a few basil leaves, and several pieces of the mozzarella, in that order. Drizzle with olive oil.

5 Once the base of the pizza has browned (about 1–2 minutes) and the crusts have puffed up a little, place the pan under the broiler until the crust takes some color. You are good to go!

Pig Cheek Vindaloo

Vindaloo may bring to mind student lads in the throes of competitive willy-waving at the local Indian restaurant, but the real thing is much more sophisticated. It originated in Goa, and the unusual use of pig cheek in a curry is attributed to Portuguese influence. The meat is marinated in a mixture of vinegar and spices overnight, then simmered slowly in a sauce and finished with a little sugar, producing a sweet and sour result that is, although still spicy, miles away from the version adapted by Western restaurants. Vindaloo does not indicate a level of heat, but rather a rich and complex dish that is even better after a couple of days in the fridge.

For the marinade

5 dried red chilies

1 tbsp cumin seeds

1 tbsp coriander seeds

1 tsp black mustard seeds

5 cloves

5 black peppercorns

10 cloves of garlic (yes)

2 fresh green chilies

½ tsp ground turmeric

5 fl oz (150 ml) red wine vinegar

2 in (5 cm) piece of fresh ginger, grated

2 tomatoes

2¼ lb (1 kg) pig cheeks (about 10 cheeks, depending on size)

Rice or bread, to serve

To make the marinade

1 In a dry frying pan, heat the red chilies, cumin seeds, coriander seeds, mustard seeds, cloves, and peppercorns for a minute or two, then grind to a paste in a spice or coffee grinder or bash in a pestle and mortar.

2 Blend the spices to a paste with the garlic, green chilies, turmeric, vinegar, ginger, and tomatoes. Mix with the pig cheeks and leave to marinate overnight in the fridge, stirring every now and then (provided you are awake, of course).

For the sauce

2 tbsp ghee or
vegetable oil

2 tsp mustard seeds

20 curry leaves

1 in (2.5 cm) piece of
cinnamon stick

2 onions, finely
chopped

1¼ pints (600 ml)
water

1 tbsp sugar

Salt

Chopped cilantro
(coriander), to garnish

Makes 4 servings

To make the sauce

1 Heat the ghee or oil in a pan large enough to hold all the meat, and add the mustard seeds, curry leaves, and cinnamon stick. When the mustard seeds start to pop, add the onions and fry until translucent.

2 Add the pig cheeks and cook until browned, then add the rest of the marinade, plus the water. Bring to the boil, turn the heat down to a simmer, and cook for 2 hours with a lid on.

3 Remove the lid and cook for a further half hour, until the meat is very tender. Add the sugar and season with salt. Sprinkle with the cilantro (coriander) and serve with rice or bread.

Marinades

You've decided to try this recipe, gone to the butcher to purchase your pig cheeks, and have got home only to realize you were supposed to marinate the meat overnight. Don't panic, it's not the end of the world! When it comes to marinades, some time is better than no time and occasionally just as effective. An hour should make a big difference to the flavor of the finished dish and a few hours will make a huge one.

CHAPTER 8

Hangovers

Seeing the Positive

Occasionally, a hangover can be almost enjoyable.
Granted, this does tend to happen more in one's
youth than in later years, but never dismiss the
possibility, because—as we all know through grim,
bitter experience—the type of hangover that
presents itself often appears to be down to luck.
We've all said it: "I ate a bag of potatoes then went
out and had a mere two glasses of wine and I feel
like shit this morning!"; or, at the other end of the
scale: "I drank two bottles of wine, four Fernet
Brancas, a yard of ale, and three shots of Jäger and
I can barely feel it this morning! In fact, I feel
great!!" In the latter case, I hate to break it to you,
but you're still drunk. Come back and see me
about midday and we'll talk. Well, I'll talk, you will
make moaning noises.

Pleasure in the pain

Somewhere in the middle, however, there is a hangover holy
grail, a sort of giggly, fun version of you that is carefree, floaty,
and funny. It's almost, almost enjoyable. You can basically eat
anything you want on that hangover—the world is your oyster
(incidentally, oysters are marvelous for sorting you out the

morning after: there's a recipe on page 113, and if you don't fancy that, I can recommend six straight up with lemon and Tabasco). Anyway, if you find yourself blessed with an "eater," then it's time to decide which of my preferred three hangover food groups you want to try. These three groups are bacon, eggs, and pancakes. There is a fourth, the sweet, but that comes later, and we don't want to get ahead of ourselves now, do we? A hangover needs careful handling. Think of the task as if you're taming a particularly ferocious beast: tread carefully at all times because it is very easy to lose control of the situation.

Many of you may be wondering where the full English breakfast features in all this. I'm sorry, but you won't find one here. It's just too much food on one plate for me, and not all of it is even that nice (see the insipid abomination that is the grilled tomato). Sure, take some of the elements—the mushrooms, the blood sausage (black pudding), the sausage—and you can make a nice breakfast, but all of it on one plate? It's a car wreck of a meal in my opinion, a vast number of ingredients all together on one plate, and all of them rather similar. There's no contrast, no respite, no let up on the forcing down of grease and salt and fat, and I am no stranger to all three of those. It's a controversial stance, granted, but I'm sticking with it.

The Solutions

So here are some of my favorite hangover cures, to be employed in the absence of cold pizza or leftover curry from the night before, which everyone knows are the greatest hangover cures of all time and not to be messed with.

The bacon sandwich

The bacon sandwich is surely one of the most popular morning-after options. The smell of sizzling bacon fat is so powerful, its consumption so restorative, that its role in the hungover cook's repertoire cannot be overstated. There is, however, a right way to make a bacon sandwich. In fact, there are a few right ways, depending on how far you want to go with the embellishments. An "embellished bacon sandwich" would, of course, include the BLT (bacon, lettuce, tomato), or my personal favorite, the SBLAT (scallion/spring onion, bacon, lettuce, avocado, tomato), but those sandwiches are not our concern here. Our most pressing aim is to nail the basics of this most glorious of breakfasts (or lunches or dinners). Bacon sandwiches are a true superfood, I tell you. Goji berries can go do one.

I shall illustrate the wrong way to make a bacon sandwich by way of an example I was served in a café in south London.

I shudder to recall the experience, but will selflessly do so for the sake of education. Firstly, the bread. It was brown. Brown. A staggeringly poor decision, because brown bread tastes healthy and delivers healthy, and healthy should be nowhere near my bacon sandwich. There are many choices of acceptable bread, ranging from the cheap, pappy white stuff, à la greasy-spoon "caff" or crappy diner, right up to the lovingly made sourdough, sturdy of crumb and sharp of crust. All have their place, and all are white.

Next, the bacon itself. The poor bacon! It had been pre-cooked (yeah, I get the idea, busy breakfast service and all that) and then reheated, probably in a microwave, to the perfect stage of flab. Everyone knows that bacon needs to be crisp. The fat should be sizzling, spitting, and actually irresistible, to the point where you would hurt someone to get at it. When cooking bacon at home, the best way to achieve perfect results is to cook it low and slow. That means medium-low heat in a skillet, which should produce a nice even result. Needless to say, the bacon should be of the best possible quality. A cooking method cannot transform a crappy ingredient. I've said it before and I'll say it again: recipes are not magic spells. My personal preference is for thick-cut treacle-cured streaky bacon. Streaky bacon has more fat and is therefore better. US readers, I sense your furrowed brows, but do not fear—your bacon is all streaky. Oh, and there must be a minimum of five slices per sandwich. MINIMUM.

And so to the sauce. The café in question twisted the knife a final time by saucing my sandwich with ketchup, when I had asked for brown sauce (steak sauce). To my mind, ketchup is for burgers and hot dogs, and nothing else. Oh, apart from fries. In a bacon sandwich, the spicy, vinegared twangle of brown sauce is king. The other slice of bread should be buttered, so that the hot bacon melts it here and there, and … you know what, I have to go buy some bacon right now.

A Good Bacon Sandwich

The cooking of the bacon is the most crucial part here, and I want you to resist the temptation to cook it on a high heat. The best bacon, the crispest bacon, is cooked low and slow, resulting in evenly browned fat, which is the aim of the game. Yes, you're hanging, but you really must resist, because no one wants flabby bits of fat, either on their body or in their sandwich.

6 slices smoked streaky bacon

2 slices white bread of your choice

Salted butter, at room temperature

Brown sauce (steak sauce)... or ketchup if you really must

Makes 1 sandwich

1 Broil (grill) or panfry your bacon on a low heat, for the reasons I explained above, making sure you check it regularly and reposition it as necessary. It really is worth the extra effort for properly evenly cooked bacon.

2 If you have pan-fried the bacon, dip each piece of bread into the juices in the pan before generously buttering one slice. If you have broiled the bacon, then, well, tough luck. Immediately put all the bacon into the sandwich (I once saw someone draining off the fat on kitchen paper—the horror!) and squirt the sauce on top.

3 Add the other slice of bread, cut into your preferred portions, and eat really bloody quickly. Incidentally, my preferred portions are quartered triangles. They just seem to taste better.

Eggs

Eggy wegs. Now these little buggers may actually, genuinely be capable of "curing" a hangover. They contain something called cysteine, which is what your body uses to break down acetaldehyde in the liver post-boozing. More of it can't be a bad thing, right? In any case, there is something rather soothing about cooking eggs, something rather homely and Sunday morning-ish about it. Cooking eggs seems to start off a chain of events that includes putting on slippers, buying a paper, smoking a pipe, turning on the wireless, going back in time …

The Perfect Egg Mayo Sandwich

There is something very comforting about the egg mayo sandwich, and I am talking about the British egg mayo here, not the American "egg salad." The latter contains all kinds of embellishments that add crunch to the sandwich, but I think the most comforting element of the British style is the softness, the nursery-food texture. It's ideal for a hangover. The perfect egg mayo has a number of qualities that are essential if the sandwich is to work properly. Firstly, the best egg mayo is made when the eggs are still warm, which is why the store-bought versions can never be as satisfying. It goes without saying that these eggs should be of the finest quality, free-range, (obviously), and from a good breed if possible. The bread must be white, and very, very fresh. If it's even slightly stale, then it's game over. Nothing too fancy, like sourdough, either; the bread needs to be squishy and soft as a kitten. As for the mayo, homemade is best, but I do understand that this is a hangover situation, so just get some really good store-bought stuff. Seasoning must be ample, for goodness' sake: plenty of sea salt and your pepper of choice. For a very British touch, I like white pepper in mine. Leafage is another point for discussion. I think watercress is the only option, and it really does need to be chopped, roughly, or big long pieces will flap out of the sandwich and onto your chin. And so we come to the embellishments. This is something I've thought long and hard about. I've tried many different combinations—scallion (spring onion), capers, gherkins, etc., etc., but as I've already said, simplicity is important here. Eventually I've come to the conclusion that the acidity one desires from additions like capers is better provided as a seasoning on the leaves, in the form of malt vinegar. Again, it doesn't get more British than that. Whatever happens, the eggs should be the main flavor.

2 tbsp mayonnaise (if you can face making your own, see recipe on page 65)

2 eggs

A small handful of watercress

Malt vinegar

White pepper (or black if you prefer)

2 slices soft white bread

Makes 1 sandwich

1 Fill a pan with cold water and put the eggs in it. Bring to the boil and cook for 6 minutes. Plunge the eggs into cold water, then peel when cool enough to handle.

2 Smoosh the hard-boiled eggs with the salt and pepper, and a few drops of malt vinegar. Don't over smoosh—you don't want a paste. Taste the mix and season again if necessary.

3 Spread this mixture generously onto one side of the bread and top with watercress. Sandwich together with a second slice of bread. Eat.

Baghdad Eggs

I first made this version of Baghdad eggs about four years ago, and it really stuck. This is where you're going to get all busy with that spiced butter. Some people find the idea of mint with eggs weird, but it's easy to leave out, or replace with cilantro (coriander). Personally, I think the mint brings a pleasing freshness to the dish.

2 generous pats (knobs) of butter

1 medium onion, diced

1 clove of garlic, crushed

Juice of ½ lemon

2 eggs

Ground cumin

Hot paprika

2 pita breads

Salt and freshly ground black pepper

Yogurt and chopped fresh mint, to garnish

Makes 2 servings

1 Melt a pat (knob) of butter in a frying pan and cook the onion gently until it starts to soften. Add the garlic and cook for a couple of minutes.

2 Squeeze in the lemon juice, then crack in the eggs. Dust each egg with a little cumin and paprika (use your fingers to do this, and be conservative—you don't want huge clumps of spice in there) plus some salt and pepper, then put a lid on and cook until the eggs are just set.

3 Toast the pita breads whole, then split them apart and toast the insides under the broiler (grill).

4 In another small pan, melt the rest of the butter and sprinkle a little extra cumin and paprika into it. Leave this on a low heat to get a little brown and nutty.

5 When the eggs are cooked, cut up the pita and arrange on a plate. Put an egg on top, making sure to get plenty of the onions too. Drizzle with some of the spiced butter and garnish with a dollop of yogurt and some mint.

Turkish-ish Eggs with Sausage

Turkish eggs are served with natural yogurt, which has the bonus effect of making everything feel healthy. This wonderful dish somehow manages to feel at once unfamiliar and very comforting, no matter how many times I eat it. Turkish eggs are usually made with a spiced butter, but I use a sausage with a very high fat content, which lets loose its glorious fat during cooking; this can then be poured over the yogurt for a wonderful visual contrast. Of course it tastes bloody good too.

2 cloves of garlic, peeled

Turkish chili flakes, to taste

Greek-style natural yogurt

A squeeze of lemon juice

2 sausages with a high fat content (I like pastirma), meat squeezed from the casing

2 scallions (spring onions), white and green parts finely sliced

2 duck or hen's eggs

A sprig of fresh flat-leaf parsley or chives, finely chopped

Salt and freshly ground black pepper

Warm bread, to serve

Makes 2 servings

1 Put the garlic cloves in a small pan and cover with water. Bring to the boil and boil for 1 minute. Drain.

2 In a pestle and mortar, mush up the blanched garlic with the chili flakes and salt to taste. Add this to a bowl along with the yogurt and lemon juice and give it a good mix, sort of whipping it lightly. Divide between two serving bowls.

3 Heat a pan of water ready for the poached eggs. In a small frying pan, gently cook the sausage meat, breaking it up, until it starts to release its fat, then add the white parts of the scallions (spring onions). If you're not using the sausage, just soften the scallions gently in a little butter or olive oil.

4 Put the eggs on to poach. By the time they are done, the sausage meat should be crisp in parts and the pan filled with lovely golden oil. Plonk a poached egg into each bowl of yogurt and top each with some of the sausage and onion mixture, the green scallion parts and the herbs. Add a little more salt and pepper, perhaps, and eat immediately with good bread and a feeling of vague shame.

Something different

Here are a couple of recipes from further afield that are a bit different from your typical egg or bacon staples.

Australian Corn Fritters with Guacamole

These are very easy to make, and they have that sweet and savory thing going on that is incredibly moreish. Serve them with bacon if you like that kind of thing (I like that kind of thing), and perhaps a splurge of guacamole on the side. It's a very Aussie brunchy vibe.

For the fritters

10 oz (280 g) (drained weight) canned sweetcorn kernels

1 egg

2 oz (60 g) all-purpose (plain) flour

½ tsp baking powder

2 scallions (spring onions), finely shredded

½ tsp smoked paprika

Vegetable oil, for frying

Salt and freshly ground black pepper

For the guacamole

¼ red onion, finely chopped

½–1 red chili, to taste

1 ripe avocado

Juice of a lime, or to taste

Cilantro (coriander) leaves

Salt and freshly ground black pepper

Makes 12 fritters

To make the fritters

1 Mix all the fritter ingredients and season generously with salt and pepper.

2 Heat a tablespoon or so of oil in a frying pan. Drop heaped spoonfuls of corn mixture into the pan, flatten, and cook for 1 minute on each side.

3 Serve with crisp bacon (see instructions on properly cooking bacon under "Bacon Sandwich," page 99), chili sauce, or guacamole, or all three.

Here's the quick guacamole recipe if you're feeling enthusiastic

1 In a pestle and mortar, give the onion and chili a bit of a bash. Sling in the avocado and continue to mash (don't make it too smooth).

2 Add lime juice and salt and pepper, and stir in the cilantro (coriander).

Fritter and Twisted

Here's a few suggestions to pimp those fritters:

- Add habanero or scotch bonnet chili if you like more heat

- Serve them with chorizo, or melted 'nduja sausage

- Add a bit of salt fish to the mix

- Add some teeny shrimp or prawns

Korean Pancakes

I first came across these pancakes when I was searching for recipes that use scallions (spring onions), of which I consume a vast amount. They're simple to make, but I must urge you not to worry at the stage when you're dipping them, whole, into the batter and trying to spread them out in the pan; yes, it looks a terrible mess, but it will cook up into a dream, I promise. I can tell you don't believe me, so you'll just have to try them. This is one of my favorite hangover recipes.

For the dipping sauce

2 tbsp soy sauce

1 tbsp rice vinegar

1 clove of garlic

1 tbsp sesame oil

1 red chili

A pinch of sugar

For the panckaes

2 oz (60 g) all-purpose (plain) flour

¼ pint (120 ml) water

A pinch of superfine (caster) sugar

A pinch of salt

1 egg

2 tbsp oil

6 scallions (spring onions), split lengthways

Makes 1–2 servings

1 First make the dipping sauce. Mix all the ingredients in a small pan and warm gently, stirring, until the sugar has dissolved. Set aside.

2 Mix the flour, water, sugar, and salt until you have a smooth batter. In a separate bowl, lightly beat the egg. Heat the oil in a large frying pan.

3 Grab the scallions (spring onions) with tongs and coat them in the batter, then put into the hot oil and spread out flat. You may need to do this in two batches. The aim is to have them covering the bottom of the pan in a single layer more or less.

4 Smoosh the scallions down in the pan with the tongs, then drizzle the remaining batter on top to fill in the gaps. Squiggle the beaten egg on top.

5 After a few minutes, when golden brown on the bottom, flip the pancake(s) and cook until golden brown on the other side. Remove from the heat, cut into wedges and serve with the dipping sauce.

Dessert

Because obviously that's what you have after breakfast...

Emergency Chocolate Croissants

I wanted to get some banana into these for their potassium content (good for a hangover, apparently), but the idea of hot banana was so repulsive to me that you're just going to have to put it in there without my knowledge, or eat the damn thing on the side. Sorry—I struggle with bananas.

1 pack ready-made puff pastry

Chocolate spread (such as Nutella)

Chopped hazelnuts

1 egg, lightly beaten

Makes 4–6 servings

1 Preheat the oven to 325°F (170°C/Gas 3). Roll out the puff pastry until it is about ⅟₁₆ in. (2 mm) thick. Cut into rectangles of about 8 x 4 in. (20 x 10 cm), then cut each rectangle across the diagonal into two triangles.

2 Place a tablespoon of chocolate spread on the long-sided end of each triangle, sprinkle with nuts, then roll up toward the pointy end, making sure the chocolate is tucked in as you go. It doesn't really matter what this looks like, to be honest—as long as you seal the chocolate inside the pastry it is going to be good.

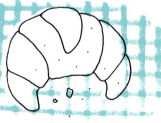

3 Brush the tops with the beaten egg. Place on a baking sheet and bake for 20 minutes, or until puffy and golden.

CHAPTER 9

Chefs

Booze Hounds

Chefs tend to have a reputation for liking a drink, or five. This may not be representative of every chef, of course, but it's certainly true of a few I know. Think about it: they're professional cooks—these are the people you want on your side the morning after. I contacted some of the country's best chefs (read: called in a few favors from my mates) to bring you a collection of frankly rather brilliant recipes, although, sadly, all but one come from men. Do female chefs drink less? Are they more secretive about their recipes? Do I just know fewer women!? Don't tax yourself with these conundrums, reader, you are far, far too hungover.

Fergus Henderson

The first man I thought of was the mighty Fergus Henderson, British chef and founder of St. John restaurant in London, famous for his nose-to-tail approach to cooking animals and, importantly for us, his fondness for Fernet Branca as solution for hangovers.

❝ I'm not sure being famous for hangover cures is the most flattering way I have been described, although I do admit to having an interest in restoring the battered frame so it can face another day. The purest solution is a healthy measure of Fernet Branca straight up. Once it is in the body you can follow its route through your system, putting to sleep any troubled organ in its path, and as far as the head goes it will certainly improve the humors. **❞**

Fergus Henderson

I have to say I agree with him, but I must tell you that Fernet is an acquired taste, and I know far more people who loathe it than who love it. A blend of many different herbs and spices, it was originally invented as a stomach medicine, which I suppose gives weight to the idea of it having a restorative effect. It is at once herbal, bitter, and sweet, and to taste it is to quite an experience. In short, this is not a cure for the novice, but should one make it past the initial shock stage, I can vouch for the efficacy of a morning shot.

Neil Rankin

Neil Rankin is a BBQ chef with a classical background. He runs the restaurant Smokehouse N1 in London, and was previously head chef at the immensely popular restaurants Pitt Cue and John Salt, also in London. He really is king of the grill, and I've also known him to sink a drink or two. I have to admire his approach in the recipe below: straight back in with the hair of the dog that bit him.

Buttered Bourbon Coffee

2 tbsp clarified grass-fed butter or ghee, chilled (grass-fed butter is widely available—try President or Kerrygold)

1 espresso

3¼ fl oz (100 ml) hot water

1¾ fl oz (50 ml) bourbon

1 If you want to clarify the butter yourself, melt it gently over a low heat, constantly skimming the scum from the surface. Once it is simmering, just keep removing all the scum until it looks clear. It takes ages, about 20–30 mins; up to you. Strain it through a sieve and try to leave the white milky bits at the bottom behind in the pan. Leave to cool.

2 Brew the espresso, then add the hot water and cold clarified butter. For the drink to work, it must be grass-fed butter. This is the secret not only to supplying your body with the right nutrients, but also to boosting the coffee so that it doesn't bring you up then drop you like a stone. Don't ask me for the science—just trust me. It works.

3 Blitz to a creamy consistency in a blender, then add the bourbon at the end. The result is an unshakable high combined with a hair-of-the-dog kick that is best enjoyed with a filthy bacon sandwich (see page 99).

Daniel Doherty

Dan is executive chef at London's Duck & Waffle, one of the few places that manage to combine great food with a kick-ass view (it's on the 40th floor). The restaurant is famous for its—all together now—duck and waffle dish (the ox cheek doughnuts are also pretty special), and it's the kind of place you could find yourself either drunk or hungover, being as it is open 24 hours a day.

" Someone told me that if you eat oysters first thing when waking up, you will be cured of the night before. I didn't for one second think it would work—it sounds gross—but, having been in a pretty bad way, with nowhere to turn, I gave it a go. All I can say is that I had the best day ever at work afterward, which says a lot to me, and it would have been even better if I had a kicky Bloody Mary to wash it down with. You'll notice bacon and blood sausage (black pudding) in the ingredients. Vital that you include them. Vital. "

Hangover Oysters

3 slices bacon, cut into lardons

2 in (5 cm) piece of blood sausage (black pudding), crumbled

1 small shallot, finely chopped

¼ tsp finely chopped red chili

1 oz (30 g) butter

A pinch of capers, roughly chopped

Juice of ½ lemon

A splash of Tabasco sauce

A pinch of chopped parsley

6 oysters, shucked

1 In a frying pan, cook the bacon until crisp.

2 Add the blood sausage (black pudding), shallot, and chili. Cook for a minute or two, then add the butter and capers, and allow the butter to turn golden brown.

3 Add the lemon juice and Tabasco, followed by the parsley. Spoon over the oysters, and get cured.

Tom Oldroyd

Tom is chef director of London's Polpo restaurants. Here are his, er, 15 steps guaranteed to banish any hangover.

Guaranteed Full Resurrection in an Hour

1 Fill and switch on kettle.

2 Dissolve 2 non-specifically branded soluble vitamin C tablets in a pint of water. With this take one paracetamol and one ibuprofen tablet.

3 Make a strong cup of tea. It is advisable to take a spoonful of sugar with this, even if you don't usually.

4 Put a small frying pan on to heat very gently with a pat (knob) of butter and a little vegetable oil.

5 Whisk 3 best-quality eggs with a pinch of salt and pepper.

6 Take a long swig of both the non-specifically branded vitamin C drink and the tea.

7 Pour the eggs into the warm pan and gently stir until they start to thicken.

8 Using a spatula, make sure the egg mix does not stick to the pan.

9 Sprinkle over some mature cheddar, thinly sliced ham, and a sliced jalapeño pepper (diced fresh chili or chili flakes are also acceptable).

10 Turn off the heat and place a plate over the pan to cover.

11 Take a tall glass and fill with 1 fl oz (25 ml) gin (or vodka if you prefer), the juice of quarter of a lemon, a good splash of Worcestershire sauce, and a few drops of Tabasco sauce. Add ice, stir, and top with tomato juice.

1 2 Finish your tea and non-specifically branded vitamin C drink.

1 3 Using the spatula, fold over your wobbly runny gooey pale omelet and slide onto the warm plate used to cover the pan.

1 4 Take omelet, Bloody Mary, fork, and comforter/duvet to your happy place, (television room/ balcony/garden/bed) and demolish. Take care not to eat too quickly, though.

1 5 Take a 40-minute nap and you will be ready to face the day.

❝ *It is possible to swap some of these components with the following foodstuffs; canned sardines on toast with salad cream (or mayo mixed with a dash of vinegar and mustard for those poor souls who can't buy salad cream locally), leftover pizza with salad cream, a fried-egg sandwich (on untoasted cheap white bread) with brown sauce (steak sauce) or salad cream, ice cream, lemonade, iced tea, coffee, sausages, cheesy pasta.* **❞**

William Leigh

William Leigh is the co-owner of Wishbone, the UK's first free-range fried chicken restaurant. He's also a product developer for some of the country's biggest supermarkets. I've known Will for a while, and we both agreed that had he not written a recipe for a rip-off "Mack" Muffin, then I damn well would have done. We see eye-to-eye when it comes to these important matters.

" Everyone loves a Sausage and Egg McMuffin from the Golden Arches. If you don't, you're either a vegetarian (poor you) or beyond saving. This is my version—a little bit of heat will help get rid of that sore bonce.

Tonkatsu sauce is the brown spiced sauce traditionally served with katsu (most commonly fried pork cutlets) in Japan. You could opt for sriracha, the most famous spicy sauce from Asia, and a favorite of most chefs. I love the brown sauce, though—really similar to HP and steak sauce. And if you're feeling really filthy, slip in a slice of processed cheese. I don't think anyone in Asia would mind. Tonkatsu sauce is available in most Asian stores and online.

While I was working on my latest project (a bar, God help me), the Bloody Mary caused many an animated discussion. My partner in the project, Josh (creator of the famous Donkey Punch at the #meateasy), and I both loved the idea of an Asian slant to this drink, which will complement your Mack-Asian-Muffin perfectly and leave you ready to go again after the last slurp. "

Mack-Asian-Muffin

½ chili, or to taste

2 tbsp vinegar, preferably rice

1 decent sausage

1 egg

Half a scallion (spring onion), finely sliced, white and green parts mixed

A large pinch of cilantro (coriander), roughly chopped

A dash of fish sauce

1 English muffin

A quarter of a lime

Tonkatsu sauce, sriracha, or brown sauce (optional)

1 slice processed cheese (optional)

Groundnut (peanut) oil, for frying

Makes 1 serving

1 Finely slice the chili and add it to the vinegar. Set aside.

2 Remove the sausage from its skin and shape into a patty. Get a frying pan up to a medium heat, drizzle in some groundnut (peanut) oil, and fry the patty until golden on both sides.

3 Meanwhile, whisk the egg and add the finely sliced scallion (spring onion), cilantro (coriander), and fish sauce.

4 Remove the sausage patty and pour the egg mixture into the pan, tilting the pan to try and keep the egg as muffin-shaped as possible. You could do this in one of those cheffy rings if you have one, but I don't, so I just scrape the edges of the egg in with a spoon until I get the shape I want. Cover with a metal bowl or pan lid to cook the top of the egg. You could flip it if you felt like it.

5 Toast the muffin (or fry it in the sausage fat if you're feeling really terrible). Place the sausage patty in the bun, top with the egg, add a few pieces of your now quick-pickled chili, squeeze over the lime juice, and pour over whichever sauce you fancy.

6 If you are adding the cheese, put it between the egg and the sausage. Stick the top half of the muffin on and tuck in.

Asian Mary

1¾ fl oz (50 ml) vodka

7 fl oz (200 ml) tomato juice

The rest is up to you—these are all to taste:

Sriracha—as much as you like to make it HAWT

Freshly ground black pepper

Celery salt

A pinch of white sugar

Fish sauce—be generous. If you're scared, use soy sauce

A squeeze of lime juice

A dash of rice vinegar or red wine vinegar

A crispy anchovy, to garnish, if you're that way inclined

1 Place all the ingredients except the anchovy in a cocktail shaker or a blender. If you're using a shaker, add a load of ice, top, and shake.

2 Pour into a tall glass filled with ice cubes. If you're using a blender, blend the ingredients, pour over ice, and serve with a straw.

Andy Oliver

UK Masterchef finalist Andy Oliver specializes in Thai food, and here's his panacea for alcohol-induced suffering: a Thai rice soup.

❝ Here's my one of my favorite hangover dishes. It's my own version of Thai rice soup, which is slightly different from the more porridge-like congee/jok. ❞

Khao Dtom

2 pints (1 liter) light chicken stock (Asian stock or a plain Western one)

Sea salt

Light soy sauce

A pinch of white sugar

A pinch of ground white pepper

1 tbsp oyster sauce, (optional)

10½ oz (300 g) cooked jasmine rice

A few leaves of Chinese cabbage (optional)

2 or 3 eggs (duck eggs are good too)

Thinly sliced crispy pork*

Thai roasted chili powder, to taste

A small piece of ginger, peeled and cut into matchsticks

3 scallions (spring onions), finely sliced

A few cilantro (coriander) leaves

A little garlic fried in oil**

Makes 2–4 servings

1 Bring the stock to the boil, and throw in any trimmings from slicing your ginger and scallion (spring onion). Season to taste with the salt, soy sauce, sugar, pepper, and oyster sauce (if using).

2 Add the cooked rice and cabbage in large pieces (if using). Simmer gently for 15 minutes, until the rice is nice and soft and the starch begins to combine with the stock.

3 Break in the eggs and simmer for a minute or two to poach them until soft.

4 Check the seasoning and ladle into bowls, making sure each has a poached egg. Garnish with crispy pork, chili powder, ginger, scallions, cilantro (coriander), and garlic oil.

＊ To make crispy pork, boil a piece of pork belly in salted water until just tender and allow to cool (overnight in the fridge is best). Slice it into thick slices, deep- or shallow-fry until crispy and delicious, then chop up.

＊＊ To make fried garlic oil, pound a head of garlic to a coarse paste and fry in oil at a medium temperature until golden. Strain out the garlic, allow the oil to cool, and return the garlic to the oil.

Yianni Papoutsis

Yianni is cofounder of MEATLiquor, and an accidental restaurateur. I first found him in a parking lot outside an industrial estate in Peckham, southeast London, in 2009, where he was cooking incredible burgers. I couldn't believe my luck and was instantly addicted. I remember my first "bobcat," a green chili and cheese number inspired by an American restaurant called the Bobcat Bite. Back then, no one was doing decent burgers in London, and Yianni single-handedly kicked off a revolution. We've partied together a lot since those days, so I can tell you with 100% confidence that this guy has some serious hangover-kicking cooking credentials.

Yianni's Brown Butter Steak and Eggs

❝ Taking mere minutes to cook, this dish contains all the major alcohol-battling food groups: meat, carbs, fat, and salt. It's not so much a hangover breakfast as such; this is what I tend to knock together around sunrise if I haven't slept yet: D.B.C. Pierre and I tucked into it many times during the whiskey-fueled all-nighters we pulled writing The MEATliquor Chronicles. ❞

3½ oz (100 g) fillet steak

2 eggs

8½ oz (250 g) butter

1 thick slice white bread

Salt and freshly ground black pepper

Makes 1 serving

1 Salt the steak thoroughly and leave, uncovered, in the fridge for an hour. After that time, scrape away any salt left visible on the steak, and pat dry with a paper towel.

2 Crack one egg into a teacup, and add just the yolk of the second, discarding the second egg white.

3 In a heavy frying pan (preferably cast iron), heat 2¾ oz (75 g) of the butter until it melts and starts to go brown. Give the steak a good grind of black pepper then fry quickly in the pan. This should take only a minute or so per side.

4 Remove the steak from the pan and set aside to rest. Add another 2¾ oz (75 g) butter to the pan. When it starts to brown, tip the pan slightly so that the butter pools, and gently lower the egg mixture into the butter. It should cook very quickly—remove it as soon as the white has cooked, but while the yolks are still runny.

5 Add the remaining butter to the pan and fry the bread until golden brown on both sides. Pour any remaining butter over the steak, and serve with a Red Snapper (see page 81) and black coffee.

Kerstin Rodgers

Kerstin Rodgers was the pioneer of supper clubs, pop-ups, night markets, and the underground dining scene in the UK. She doesn't drink much nowadays, but that doesn't mean she didn't earn her credentials fair and bloody square back in the day. I've never known a woman with so many brilliant stories. Here's one of them:

> **❝** I discovered quesadillas as a hangover remedy when I was illegally living and working in Los Angeles in my early twenties. I'd gone in on a tourist visa, then just stayed. I made up a social security number; this was before the days of computerization, so it was no problem. I even pretended that I had 7 children to pay less tax which, considering I was only 21, would have been quite incredible. But nobody questioned it. I was working in a photo lab and every morning a food truck would pull up outside selling Mexican food. Their quesadilla was a miracle of fat and carbs and the hedonic high of a spicy sauce. **❞**

Cheesy Quesadilla

3½ oz (100 g) Monterey Jack, medium cheddar, or queso fresco cheese

2 flour tortillas

Half an avocado, sliced ½ in. (1 cm) thick

A few drops of hot jalapeño sauce and a few cilantro (coriander) leaves (optional), to garnish

Makes 1 serving

1 For ideal melting consistency, grate the cheese. Sprinkle it all over one of the tortillas, dot the avocado around, then place the other tortilla over it.

2 To cook, put it in the microwave (I'm being kind—I know you are feeling awful, so the easier the method the better) and nuke it for a minute, just enough for the cheese to melt but not to cook the avocado. If you don't have a microwave, put a dry frying pan on a medium heat, let the bottom warm up, then place the quesadilla on it. Cook for approximately 1 minute each side.

3 Serve with the chili sauce and, if you can be bothered, a few fresh cilantro (coriander) leaves.

In Closing

That's it, readers. I've done all I can; you're on your own now. I share below some suggestions for further reading, should you feel the need to continue your bender. I shall leave you with this quote from (as ever) one of my mates.

> *"My parents once microwaved a chicken.*
> *They weren't drunk, but I think it deserves*
> *a mention anyway."*

Cheers!

Further Reading:

Other stuff written by me:

Food Stories blog (helengraves.co.uk)

The London Review of Sandwiches blog
    (londonreviewofsandwiches.wordpress.com)

101 Sandwiches (Dog 'n' Bone, 2013)

Cook Your Date Into Bed (Dog 'n' Bone, 2014)

Stuff written by other people:

Kingsley Amis, *Everyday Drinking* (Bloomsbury, 2008)

Dale DeGroff, *The Craft of The Cocktail* (Proof, 2003)

Mark Dredge, *Craft Beer World* (Dog 'n' Bone, 2013)

Seb Emina and Malcolm Eggs, *The Breakfast Bible*
    (Bloomsbury, 2013)

F. Scott Fitzgerald, *On Booze* (Picador 2012)

James Hamilton-Paterson, *Cooking with Fernet Branca* (Faber
    & Faber, 2005)

Aeneas MacDonald, *Whisky* (1930;
    reprinted by Canongate, 2006)

Jancis Robinson and Hugh Johnson,
    World Atlas of Wine (Mitchell
    Beazley, seventh edition 2013)

Hunter S. Thompson, *The Rum Diary*
    (Bloomsbury, 1998)

David Wondrich, *Imbibe!*, (Perigee, 2007)

Index

Acknowledgments

I should like to thank the following people for their recipe contributions: Daniel Doherty for his hangover oysters; James and Thom Elliot for their frying-pan pizza; Fergus Henderson for getting back to me about Fernet Branca; William Leigh for his McAsianMuffin and Asian Mary; Tom Oldroyd for his 15 steps; Andy Oliver for his Khao Dtom; Yianni Papoutsis for his Brown Butter Steak and Eggs; Neil Rankin for his Buttered Bourbon Coffee; Kerstin Rodgers for her Cheesy Quesadilla; and Dan Vaux-Nobes for his fry sauce. Thanks to Dog 'n' Bone for commissioning me to write three books(!), and especially to Pete and Mark for being such good fun. Thank you to all my mates for continually getting drunk (and cooking) with me, and for giving me endless advice and stories (almost all of which I couldn't include because they were either too rude or too incriminating). Finally, I'd like to thank Donald for being my partner in drunken crime, as always.